Mometrix TEST PREPARATION

DSST®

Principles of Supervision Exam Secrets Study Guide

DEAR FUTURE EXAM SUCCESS STORY

First of all, **THANK YOU** for purchasing Mometrix study materials!

Second, congratulations! You are one of the few determined test-takers who are committed to doing whatever it takes to excel on your exam. **You have come to the right place.** We developed these study materials with one goal in mind: to deliver you the information you need in a format that's concise and easy to use.

In addition to optimizing your guide for the content of the test, we've outlined our recommended steps for breaking down the preparation process into small, attainable goals so you can make sure you stay on track.

We've also analyzed the entire test-taking process, identifying the most common pitfalls and showing how you can overcome them and be ready for any curveball the test throws you.

Standardized testing is one of the biggest obstacles on your road to success, which only increases the importance of doing well in the high-pressure, high-stakes environment of test day. Your results on this test could have a significant impact on your future, and this guide provides the information and practical advice to help you achieve your full potential on test day.

Your success is our success

We would love to hear from you! If you would like to share the story of your exam success or if you have any questions or comments in regard to our products, please contact us at **800-673-8175** or **support@mometrix.com**.

Thanks again for your business and we wish you continued success!

Sincerely,
The Mometrix Test Preparation Team

Need more help? Check out our flashcards at:
http://MometrixFlashcards.com/DSST

Written and edited by the Mometrix Exam Secrets Test Prep Team
Printed in the United States of America

TABLE OF CONTENTS

Introduction

Thank you for purchasing this resource! You have made the choice to prepare yourself for a test that could have a huge impact on your future, and this guide is designed to help you be fully ready for test day. Obviously, it's important to have a solid understanding of the test material, but you also need to be prepared for the unique environment and stressors of the test, so that you can perform to the best of your abilities.

For this purpose, the first section that appears in this guide is the **Secret Keys**. We've devoted countless hours to meticulously researching what works and what doesn't, and we've boiled down our findings to the five most impactful steps you can take to improve your performance on the test. We start at the beginning with study planning and move through the preparation process, all the way to the testing strategies that will help you get the most out of what you know when you're finally sitting in front of the test.

We recommend that you start preparing for your test as far in advance as possible. However, if you've bought this guide as a last-minute study resource and only have a few days before your test, we recommend that you skip over the first two Secret Keys since they address a long-term study plan.

If you struggle with **test anxiety**, we strongly encourage you to check out our recommendations for how you can overcome it. Test anxiety is a formidable foe, but it can be beaten, and we want to make sure you have the tools you need to defeat it.

Secret Key #1 – Plan Big, Study Small

There's a lot riding on your performance. If you want to ace this test, you're going to need to keep your skills sharp and the material fresh in your mind. You need a plan that lets you review everything you need to know while still fitting in your schedule. We'll break this strategy down into three categories.

Information Organization

Start with the information you already have: the official test outline. From this, you can make a complete list of all the concepts you need to cover before the test. Organize these concepts into groups that can be studied together, and create a list of any related vocabulary you need to learn so you can brush up on any difficult terms. You'll want to keep this vocabulary list handy once you actually start studying since you may need to add to it along the way.

Time Management

Once you have your set of study concepts, decide how to spread them out over the time you have left before the test. Break your study plan into small, clear goals so you have a manageable task for each day and know exactly what you're doing. Then just focus on one small step at a time. When you manage your time this way, you don't need to spend hours at a time studying. Studying a small block of content for a short period each day helps you retain information better and avoid stressing over how much you have left to do. You can relax knowing that you have a plan to cover everything in time. In order for this strategy to be effective though, you have to start studying early and stick to your schedule. Avoid the exhaustion and futility that comes from last-minute cramming!

Study Environment

The environment you study in has a big impact on your learning. Studying in a coffee shop, while probably more enjoyable, is not likely to be as fruitful as studying in a quiet room. It's important to keep distractions to a minimum. You're only planning to study for a short block of time, so make the most of it. Don't pause to check your phone or get up to find a snack. It's also important to **avoid multitasking**. Research has consistently shown that multitasking will make your studying dramatically less effective. Your study area should also be comfortable and well-lit so you don't have the distraction of straining your eyes or sitting on an uncomfortable chair.

The time of day you study is also important. You want to be rested and alert. Don't wait until just before bedtime. Study when you'll be most likely to comprehend and remember. Even better, if you know what time of day your test will be, set that time aside for study. That way your brain will be used to working on that subject at that specific time and you'll have a better chance of recalling information.

Finally, it can be helpful to team up with others who are studying for the same test. Your actual studying should be done in as isolated an environment as possible, but the work of organizing the information and setting up the study plan can be divided up. In between study sessions, you can discuss with your teammates the concepts that you're all studying and quiz each other on the details. Just be sure that your teammates are as serious about the test as you are. If you find that your study time is being replaced with social time, you might need to find a new team.

Secret Key #2 – Make Your Studying Count

You're devoting a lot of time and effort to preparing for this test, so you want to be absolutely certain it will pay off. This means doing more than just reading the content and hoping you can remember it on test day. It's important to make every minute of study count. There are two main areas you can focus on to make your studying count.

Retention

It doesn't matter how much time you study if you can't remember the material. You need to make sure you are retaining the concepts. To check your retention of the information you're learning, try recalling it at later times with minimal prompting. Try carrying around flashcards and glance at one or two from time to time or ask a friend who's also studying for the test to quiz you.

To enhance your retention, look for ways to put the information into practice so that you can apply it rather than simply recalling it. If you're using the information in practical ways, it will be much easier to remember. Similarly, it helps to solidify a concept in your mind if you're not only reading it to yourself but also explaining it to someone else. Ask a friend to let you teach them about a concept you're a little shaky on (or speak aloud to an imaginary audience if necessary). As you try to summarize, define, give examples, and answer your friend's questions, you'll understand the concepts better and they will stay with you longer. Finally, step back for a big picture view and ask yourself how each piece of information fits with the whole subject. When you link the different concepts together and see them working together as a whole, it's easier to remember the individual components.

Finally, practice showing your work on any multi-step problems, even if you're just studying. Writing out each step you take to solve a problem will help solidify the process in your mind, and you'll be more likely to remember it during the test.

Modality

Modality simply refers to the means or method by which you study. Choosing a study modality that fits your own individual learning style is crucial. No two people learn best in exactly the same way, so it's important to know your strengths and use them to your advantage.

For example, if you learn best by visualization, focus on visualizing a concept in your mind and draw an image or a diagram. Try color-coding your notes, illustrating them, or creating symbols that will trigger your mind to recall a learned concept. If you learn best by hearing or discussing information, find a study partner who learns the same way or read aloud to yourself. Think about how to put the information in your own words. Imagine that you are giving a lecture on the topic and record yourself so you can listen to it later.

For any learning style, flashcards can be helpful. Organize the information so you can take advantage of spare moments to review. Underline key words or phrases. Use different colors for different categories. Mnemonic devices (such as creating a short list in which every item starts with the same letter) can also help with retention. Find what works best for you and use it to store the information in your mind most effectively and easily.

Secret Key #3 – Practice the Right Way

Your success on test day depends not only on how many hours you put into preparing, but also on whether you prepared the right way. It's good to check along the way to see if your studying is paying off. One of the most effective ways to do this is by taking practice tests to evaluate your progress. Practice tests are useful because they show exactly where you need to improve. Every time you take a practice test, pay special attention to these three groups of questions:

- The questions you got wrong
- The questions you had to guess on, even if you guessed right
- The questions you found difficult or slow to work through

This will show you exactly what your weak areas are, and where you need to devote more study time. Ask yourself why each of these questions gave you trouble. Was it because you didn't understand the material? Was it because you didn't remember the vocabulary? Do you need more repetitions on this type of question to build speed and confidence? Dig into those questions and figure out how you can strengthen your weak areas as you go back to review the material.

Additionally, many practice tests have a section explaining the answer choices. It can be tempting to read the explanation and think that you now have a good understanding of the concept. However, an explanation likely only covers part of the question's broader context. Even if the explanation makes perfect sense, **go back and investigate** every concept related to the question until you're positive you have a thorough understanding.

As you go along, keep in mind that the practice test is just that: practice. Memorizing these questions and answers will not be very helpful on the actual test because it is unlikely to have any of the same exact questions. If you only know the right answers to the sample questions, you won't be prepared for the real thing. **Study the concepts** until you understand them fully, and then you'll be able to answer any question that shows up on the test.

It's important to wait on the practice tests until you're ready. If you take a test on your first day of study, you may be overwhelmed by the amount of material covered and how much you need to learn. Work up to it gradually.

On test day, you'll need to be prepared for answering questions, managing your time, and using the test-taking strategies you've learned. It's a lot to balance, like a mental marathon that will have a big impact on your future. Like training for a marathon, you'll need to start slowly and work your way up. When test day arrives, you'll be ready.

Start with the strategies you've read in the first two Secret Keys—plan your course and study in the way that works best for you. If you have time, consider using multiple study resources to get different approaches to the same concepts. It can be helpful to see difficult concepts from more than one angle. Then find a good source for practice tests. Many times, the test website will suggest potential study resources or provide sample tests.

Practice Test Strategy

If you're able to find at least three practice tests, we recommend this strategy:

Untimed and Open-Book Practice

Take the first test with no time constraints and with your notes and study guide handy. Take your time and focus on applying the strategies you've learned.

Timed and Open-Book Practice

Take the second practice test open-book as well, but set a timer and practice pacing yourself to finish in time.

Timed and Closed-Book Practice

Take any other practice tests as if it were test day. Set a timer and put away your study materials. Sit at a table or desk in a quiet room, imagine yourself at the testing center, and answer questions as quickly and accurately as possible.

Keep repeating timed and closed-book tests on a regular basis until you run out of practice tests or it's time for the actual test. Your mind will be ready for the schedule and stress of test day, and you'll be able to focus on recalling the material you've learned.

Secret Key #4 – Pace Yourself

Once you're fully prepared for the material on the test, your biggest challenge on test day will be managing your time. Just knowing that the clock is ticking can make you panic even if you have plenty of time left. Work on pacing yourself so you can build confidence against the time constraints of the exam. Pacing is a difficult skill to master, especially in a high-pressure environment, so **practice is vital**.

Set time expectations for your pace based on how much time is available. For example, if a section has 60 questions and the time limit is 30 minutes, you know you have to average 30 seconds or less per question in order to answer them all. Although 30 seconds is the hard limit, set 25 seconds per question as your goal, so you reserve extra time to spend on harder questions. When you budget extra time for the harder questions, you no longer have any reason to stress when those questions take longer to answer.

Don't let this time expectation distract you from working through the test at a calm, steady pace, but keep it in mind so you don't spend too much time on any one question. Recognize that taking extra time on one question you don't understand may keep you from answering two that you do understand later in the test. If your time limit for a question is up and you're still not sure of the answer, mark it and move on, and come back to it later if the time and the test format allow. If the testing format doesn't allow you to return to earlier questions, just make an educated guess; then put it out of your mind and move on.

On the easier questions, be careful not to rush. It may seem wise to hurry through them so you have more time for the challenging ones, but it's not worth missing one if you know the concept and just didn't take the time to read the question fully. Work efficiently but make sure you understand the question and have looked at all of the answer choices, since more than one may seem right at first.

Even if you're paying attention to the time, you may find yourself a little behind at some point. You should speed up to get back on track, but do so wisely. Don't panic; just take a few seconds less on each question until you're caught up. Don't guess without thinking, but do look through the answer choices and eliminate any you know are wrong. If you can get down to two choices, it is often worthwhile to guess from those. Once you've chosen an answer, move on and don't dwell on any that you skipped or had to hurry through. If a question was taking too long, chances are it was one of the harder ones, so you weren't as likely to get it right anyway.

On the other hand, if you find yourself getting ahead of schedule, it may be beneficial to slow down a little. The more quickly you work, the more likely you are to make a careless mistake that will affect your score. You've budgeted time for each question, so don't be afraid to spend that time. Practice an efficient but careful pace to get the most out of the time you have.

Secret Key #5 – Have a Plan for Guessing

When you're taking the test, you may find yourself stuck on a question. Some of the answer choices seem better than others, but you don't see the one answer choice that is obviously correct. What do you do?

The scenario described above is very common, yet most test takers have not effectively prepared for it. Developing and practicing a plan for guessing may be one of the single most effective uses of your time as you get ready for the exam.

In developing your plan for guessing, there are three questions to address:

- When should you start the guessing process?
- How should you narrow down the choices?
- Which answer should you choose?

When to Start the Guessing Process

Unless your plan for guessing is to select C every time (which, despite its merits, is not what we recommend), you need to leave yourself enough time to apply your answer elimination strategies. Since you have a limited amount of time for each question, that means that if you're going to give yourself the best shot at guessing correctly, you have to decide quickly whether or not you will guess.

Of course, the best-case scenario is that you don't have to guess at all, so first, see if you can answer the question based on your knowledge of the subject and basic reasoning skills. Focus on the key words in the question and try to jog your memory of related topics. Give yourself a chance to bring the knowledge to mind, but once you realize that you don't have (or you can't access) the knowledge you need to answer the question, it's time to start the guessing process.

It's almost always better to start the guessing process too early than too late. It only takes a few seconds to remember something and answer the question from knowledge. Carefully eliminating wrong answer choices takes longer. Plus, going through the process of eliminating answer choices can actually help jog your memory.

Summary: Start the guessing process as soon as you decide that you can't answer the question based on your knowledge.

How to Narrow Down the Choices

The next chapter in this book (**Test-Taking Strategies**) includes a wide range of strategies for how to approach questions and how to look for answer choices to eliminate. You will definitely want to read those carefully, practice them, and figure out which ones work best for you. Here though, we're going to address a mindset rather than a particular strategy.

Your odds of guessing an answer correctly depend on how many options you are choosing from.

Number of options left	5	4	3	2	1
Odds of guessing correctly	20%	25%	33%	50%	100%

You can see from this chart just how valuable it is to be able to eliminate incorrect answers and make an educated guess, but there are two things that many test takers do that cause them to miss out on the benefits of guessing:

- Accidentally eliminating the correct answer
- Selecting an answer based on an impression

We'll look at the first one here, and the second one in the next section.

To avoid accidentally eliminating the correct answer, we recommend a thought exercise called **the $5 challenge**. In this challenge, you only eliminate an answer choice from contention if you are willing to bet $5 on it being wrong. Why $5? Five dollars is a small but not insignificant amount of money. It's an amount you could afford to lose but wouldn't want to throw away. And while losing $5 once might not hurt too much, doing it twenty times will set you back $100. In the same way, each small decision you make—eliminating a choice here, guessing on a question there—won't by itself impact your score very much, but when you put them all together, they can make a big difference. By holding each answer choice elimination decision to a higher standard, you can reduce the risk of accidentally eliminating the correct answer.

The $5 challenge can also be applied in a positive sense: If you are willing to bet $5 that an answer choice *is* correct, go ahead and mark it as correct.

Summary: Only eliminate an answer choice if you are willing to bet $5 that it is wrong.

Which Answer to Choose

You're taking the test. You've run into a hard question and decided you'll have to guess. You've eliminated all the answer choices you're willing to bet $5 on. Now you have to pick an answer. Why do we even need to talk about this? Why can't you just pick whichever one you feel like when the time comes?

The answer to these questions is that if you don't come into the test with a plan, you'll rely on your impression to select an answer choice, and if you do that, you risk falling into a trap. The test writers know that everyone who takes their test will be guessing on some of the questions, so they intentionally write wrong answer choices to seem plausible. You still have to pick an answer though, and if the wrong answer choices are designed to look right, how can you ever be sure that you're not falling for their trap? The best solution we've found to this dilemma is to take the decision out of your hands entirely. Here is the process we recommend:

Once you've eliminated any choices that you are confident (willing to bet $5) are wrong, select the first remaining choice as your answer.

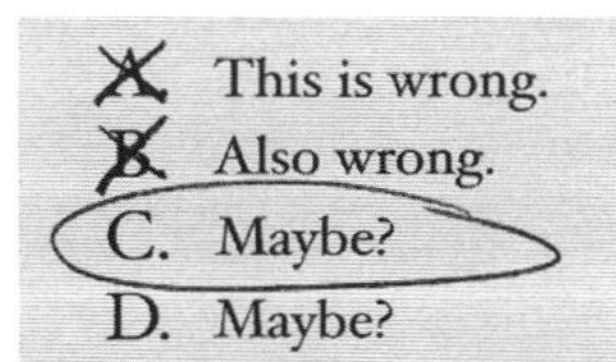

Whether you choose to select the first remaining choice, the second, or the last, the important thing is that you use some preselected standard. Using this approach guarantees that you will not be enticed into selecting an answer choice that looks right, because you are not basing your decision on how the answer choices look.

This is not meant to make you question your knowledge. Instead, it is to help you recognize the difference between your knowledge and your impressions. There's a huge difference between thinking an answer is right because of what you know, and thinking an answer is right because it looks or sounds like it should be right.

Summary: To ensure that your selection is appropriately random, make a predetermined selection from among all answer choices you have not eliminated.

Test-Taking Strategies

This section contains a list of test-taking strategies that you may find helpful as you work through the test. By taking what you know and applying logical thought, you can maximize your chances of answering any question correctly!

It is very important to realize that every question is different and every person is different: no single strategy will work on every question, and no single strategy will work for every person. That's why we've included all of them here, so you can try them out and determine which ones work best for different types of questions and which ones work best for you.

Question Strategies

✓ Read Carefully

Read the question and the answer choices carefully. Don't miss the question because you misread the terms. You have plenty of time to read each question thoroughly and make sure you understand what is being asked. Yet a happy medium must be attained, so don't waste too much time. You must read carefully and efficiently.

✓ Contextual Clues

Look for contextual clues. If the question includes a word you are not familiar with, look at the immediate context for some indication of what the word might mean. Contextual clues can often give you all the information you need to decipher the meaning of an unfamiliar word. Even if you can't determine the meaning, you may be able to narrow down the possibilities enough to make a solid guess at the answer to the question.

✓ Prefixes

If you're having trouble with a word in the question or answer choices, try dissecting it. Take advantage of every clue that the word might include. Prefixes can be a huge help. Usually, they allow you to determine a basic meaning. *Pre-* means before, *post-* means after, *pro-* is positive, *de-* is negative. From prefixes, you can get an idea of the general meaning of the word and try to put it into context.

✓ Hedge Words

Watch out for critical hedge words, such as *likely, may, can, often, almost, mostly, usually, generally, rarely*, and *sometimes*. Question writers insert these hedge phrases to cover every possibility. Often an answer choice will be wrong simply because it leaves no room for exception. Be on guard for answer choices that have definitive words such as *exactly* and *always*.

✓ Switchback Words

Stay alert for *switchbacks*. These are the words and phrases frequently used to alert you to shifts in thought. The most common switchback words are *but, although*, and *however*. Others include *nevertheless, on the other hand, even though, while, in spite of, despite*, and *regardless of*. Switchback words are important to catch because they can change the direction of the question or an answer choice.

✓ Face Value

When in doubt, use common sense. Accept the situation in the problem at face value. Don't read too much into it. These problems will not require you to make wild assumptions. If you have to go beyond creativity and warp time or space in order to have an answer choice fit the question, then you should move on and consider the other answer choices. These are normal problems rooted in reality. The applicable relationship or explanation may not be readily apparent, but it is there for you to figure out. Use your common sense to interpret anything that isn't clear.

Answer Choice Strategies

✓ Answer Selection

The most thorough way to pick an answer choice is to identify and eliminate wrong answers until only one is left, then confirm it is the correct answer. Sometimes an answer choice may immediately seem right, but be careful. The test writers will usually put more than one reasonable answer choice on each question, so take a second to read all of them and make sure that the other choices are not equally obvious. As long as you have time left, it is better to read every answer choice than to pick the first one that looks right without checking the others.

✓ Answer Choice Families

An answer choice family consists of two (in rare cases, three) answer choices that are very similar in construction and cannot all be true at the same time. If you see two answer choices that are direct opposites or parallels, one of them is usually the correct answer. For instance, if one answer choice says that quantity *x* increases and another either says that quantity *x* decreases (opposite) or says that quantity *y* increases (parallel), then those answer choices would fall into the same family. An answer choice that doesn't match the construction of the answer choice family is more likely to be incorrect. Most questions will not have answer choice families, but when they do appear, you should be prepared to recognize them.

✓ Eliminate Answers

Eliminate answer choices as soon as you realize they are wrong, but make sure you consider all possibilities. If you are eliminating answer choices and realize that the last one you are left with is also wrong, don't panic. Start over and consider each choice again. There may be something you missed the first time that you will realize on the second pass.

✓ Avoid Fact Traps

Don't be distracted by an answer choice that is factually true but doesn't answer the question. You are looking for the choice that answers the question. Stay focused on what the question is asking for so you don't accidentally pick an answer that is true but incorrect. Always go back to the question and make sure the answer choice you've selected actually answers the question and is not merely a true statement.

✓ Extreme Statements

In general, you should avoid answers that put forth extreme actions as standard practice or proclaim controversial ideas as established fact. An answer choice that states the "process should be used in certain situations, if..." is much more likely to be correct than one that states the "process should be discontinued completely." The first is a calm rational statement and doesn't even make a definitive, uncompromising stance, using a hedge word *if* to provide wiggle room, whereas the second choice is far more extreme.

⊘ BENCHMARK

As you read through the answer choices and you come across one that seems to answer the question well, mentally select that answer choice. This is not your final answer, but it's the one that will help you evaluate the other answer choices. The one that you selected is your benchmark or standard for judging each of the other answer choices. Every other answer choice must be compared to your benchmark. That choice is correct until proven otherwise by another answer choice beating it. If you find a better answer, then that one becomes your new benchmark. Once you've decided that no other choice answers the question as well as your benchmark, you have your final answer.

⊘ PREDICT THE ANSWER

Before you even start looking at the answer choices, it is often best to try to predict the answer. When you come up with the answer on your own, it is easier to avoid distractions and traps because you will know exactly what to look for. The right answer choice is unlikely to be word-for-word what you came up with, but it should be a close match. Even if you are confident that you have the right answer, you should still take the time to read each option before moving on.

General Strategies

⊘ TOUGH QUESTIONS

If you are stumped on a problem or it appears too hard or too difficult, don't waste time. Move on! Remember though, if you can quickly check for obviously incorrect answer choices, your chances of guessing correctly are greatly improved. Before you completely give up, at least try to knock out a couple of possible answers. Eliminate what you can and then guess at the remaining answer choices before moving on.

⊘ CHECK YOUR WORK

Since you will probably not know every term listed and the answer to every question, it is important that you get credit for the ones that you do know. Don't miss any questions through careless mistakes. If at all possible, try to take a second to look back over your answer selection and make sure you've selected the correct answer choice and haven't made a costly careless mistake (such as marking an answer choice that you didn't mean to mark). This quick double check should more than pay for itself in caught mistakes for the time it costs.

⊘ PACE YOURSELF

It's easy to be overwhelmed when you're looking at a page full of questions; your mind is confused and full of random thoughts, and the clock is ticking down faster than you would like. Calm down and maintain the pace that you have set for yourself. Especially as you get down to the last few minutes of the test, don't let the small numbers on the clock make you panic. As long as you are on track by monitoring your pace, you are guaranteed to have time for each question.

⊘ DON'T RUSH

It is very easy to make errors when you are in a hurry. Maintaining a fast pace in answering questions is pointless if it makes you miss questions that you would have gotten right otherwise. Test writers like to include distracting information and wrong answers that seem right. Taking a little extra time to avoid careless mistakes can make all the difference in your test score. Find a pace that allows you to be confident in the answers that you select.

⊘ KEEP MOVING

Panicking will not help you pass the test, so do your best to stay calm and keep moving. Taking deep breaths and going through the answer elimination steps you practiced can help to break through a stress barrier and keep your pace.

Final Notes

The combination of a solid foundation of content knowledge and the confidence that comes from practicing your plan for applying that knowledge is the key to maximizing your performance on test day. As your foundation of content knowledge is built up and strengthened, you'll find that the strategies included in this chapter become more and more effective in helping you quickly sift through the distractions and traps of the test to isolate the correct answer.

Now that you're preparing to move forward into the test content chapters of this book, be sure to keep your goal in mind. As you read, think about how you will be able to apply this information on the test. If you've already seen sample questions for the test and you have an idea of the question format and style, try to come up with questions of your own that you can answer based on what you're reading. This will give you valuable practice applying your knowledge in the same ways you can expect to on test day.

Good luck and good studying!

Roles and Responsibilities of the Supervisor

Supervision

There are a number of possible definitions for supervision:

- Supervision is directing the professional performance of another person.
- Supervision is leading subordinates to the accomplishment of agreed-upon goals.
- Supervision is direct guidance related to specific techniques and methods.
- Supervision is the maintenance of civility and morale among employees.
- Supervision is the instruction and training of lower-level employees.
- Supervision is facilitating communication among the various levels of management.

Levels of Management

First-line management: the bottom rung of management. These managers are in charge of employees who do not have subordinates. Among managers, they have the closest contact with the work as it is performed. They are accountable to middle or upper management, depending on the size of the firm.

Middle management: charged with administrating factories or departments. Often, middle management is in charge of first-line management, and in turn, responsible for reporting to upper management.

Upper management: the highest level of management, responsible for the overall performance of the organization. Upper management tends to leave day-to-day decisions to subordinates, focusing instead on overarching goals. These managers are responsible for reporting to ownership and the board of directors.

Supervision Styles

Directing Style

Directing style emphasizes providing direct guidance to employees. A supervisor using this style does not spend time reassuring employees, but instead provides specific, practical instruction. This technique can be useful when employees are already motivated.

Supporting Style

Supporting style emphasizes morale and team spirit among employees. This style can be a good idea when employees are skilled but uncertain of their abilities.

Coaching Style

Coaching style provides both support and practical instruction. A supervisor using this style is in constant communication with employees and provides continuous evaluation. This is a good supervision style for working with new employees.

Delegating Style

Delegating style provides little instruction or reassurance. A manager who is using this style occasionally evaluates performance, but generally leaves employees to accomplish tasks on their own.

SUPERVISION AND MANAGEMENT

There are some slight differences between supervision and management. Supervision is the direct guidance and evaluation of employees in the workplace.

Management, on the other hand, is the organization and planning of work. Supervision is a bit more "hands on" and informal. Often, employees at the same level in the organizational hierarchy will supervise one another, depending on who has more experience or knowledge of a particular task. At other times, a manager will oversee an entire company, without supervising any particular employees. In many cases, there is overlap between supervision and management.

LEADERSHIP AND MANAGEMENT

Leadership and management are similar fields, though there are some slight differences. Leadership tends to involve more attention to the morale and the emotional state of an organization. A leader sets out clear goals for the organization, and then tries to motivate employees to achieve these goals. Anyone in an organization can be a leader, although it is most common for a leader to be the chief executive officer or a manager.

Management, on the other hand, is a fine-grained, day-to-day process of leading an organization toward its goals. A manager has to pay specific attention to the resources required for a goal, and must be able to create realistic plans. The manager needs to ensure that an organization is capable of reaching its goals, and needs to monitor work performance to ensure that the organization is on track.

PROJECT MANAGER

Project manager is the employee responsible for the completion of a particular project, whether large or small.

PRODUCT MANAGER

Product manager is the employee in charge of service or product development; a product manager is usually directly involved in the nuts and bolts of manufacture.

PRODUCT LINE MANAGER

Product line manager is similar to a product manager, but responsible for multiple similar products.

FUNCTIONAL MANAGER

Functional manager is the employee in charge of a broad department within an organization. Such departments include engineering, marketing, and product development.

GENERAL MANAGER

General manager is the employee responsible for several different functional departments; for instance, the general manager of a factory is responsible for all of the different processes performed there.

MANAGEMENT DEVELOPMENT TYPES

Executive development: improves the performance of top-level managers by providing instruction in strategic planning, program development, human resources, branding, and leadership.

Leadership development: emphasizes the promotion of goals, including an emphasis on clarity and communication.

Management development: emphasizes the promotion of planning, organizing, leading, and monitoring skills.

Supervisor development: improves employees' skills in leading, instructing, and evaluating subordinates.

Successful Supervisor Skills

Successful supervisor skills in the workplace are:

- *Technical skills*: necessary so that the supervisor can provide direct instruction
- *Analytical skills*: required for solving specific problems, as well as noting changes in the work environment
- *Decision-making skills*: responsible for solving technical problems and harnessing the powers of the organization at large
- *People skills:* necessary to create good relationships with employees and among subordinates
- *Communication skills*: essential to the ability to outline plans, solve problems, and provide useful instruction; also necessary to provide good reports to management
- *Computer skills*: often required for performing evaluation and communication tasks

Supervisor Managerial Roles

Managerial roles the supervisor has:

- *Facilitator*: Supervisors provide hands-on guidance to employees
- *Monitor*: Supervisors evaluate performance and correct problems
- *Leader*: Supervisors create motivation, manage personnel problems, and influence human resources decisions
- *Liaison*: Supervisors create communication links among employees
- *Spokesperson*: Supervisors advocate for their departments in their reports to their superiors
- *Disseminator*: Supervisors explain managerial decisions to subordinate employees
- *Negotiator*: Supervisors advocate for better working conditions and pay
- *Resource allocator*: Supervisors decide how to spend time, money, and manpower
- *Disturbance handler*: Supervisors resolve technical problems and personal conflicts
- *Entrepreneur*: Supervisors innovate to improve production methods and performance

Organizational Roles

Within an organization, employees inhabit different roles. A role is a set of expectations about how the employee will behave. Information about the role that is generated by the organization is called the "sent" role. How the employee interprets that information is called the "received" role. The actual performance of the role is called the "enacted" role. There are a number of ways for organizational role conflict to occur:

- *Inter-role conflict*: an employee who inhabits two different roles finds these roles coming into conflict.
- *Intra-role conflict*: two different sets of employees have divergent interests; for instance, the desire of management for greater profits conflicts with the desire of employees for better wages.

- *Inter-sender conflict*: one part of an organization communicates conflicting messages about roles; for instance, management tells employees to produce more but to avoid working overtime.
- *Person-role conflict*: a person finds that the performance of their job conflicts with their personal beliefs.

Role ambiguity, in which the parameters of a role are unclear, is another potential problem in organizations. Also, if a single person is given too many tasks, he or she may experience role overload.

Business Ethics in General

Ethics are general provisions regarding right and wrong behavior. In business, there is a specific set of ethics related to the performance of work tasks and the communication within and by an organization. For instance, businesses should seek to improve the communities in which they live, rather than exploit resources and people. This aspect of business ethics is known as social responsibility. In order for the provisions of business ethics to have value, they must be drafted by the employees and management, and acceptable to the community at large. Sometimes, ethical issues in business are shrouded in ambiguity. It is the job of a supervisor, in many cases, to clarify murky ethical issues.

Business Environment Impacts Ethics

Every day a business manager must confront some issue of ethics. Many of the forces that drive capitalism are at odds with the human values of generosity and fairness. For this reason, managers must constantly guard against unethical conduct. For instance, in some cases the personal desires of an employee will come into contact with the desires of the organization as a whole. This conflict of interest can lead to fraud. Other times, employees will offer or be offered unfair inducements in what is known as bribery. It is important for an organization to establish specific, well-documented rules of conduct, and then to enforce these rules. A code of ethics should be easy for lawyers to access and understand.

Organization Influences

Even when the ethical rules of an organization are clear and well known, a climate of disobedience and immoral behavior will erode the standards of employees. It is absolutely essential for management and supervisors to set a good example. Also, any transgressions should be punished publicly, so that employees will understand the consequences of violating the code of ethics. However, it is also important to publicly reward ethical behavior. The maintenance of sound business ethics requires constant vigilance by management.

Multicultural Identity

A ceremony or act that indicates an individual's entry into a new phase of life is called a rite of passage. Many cultures have covert rites of passage, as for instance the vision quest endured by Native American youths on their entry to adulthood. Rites of passage could also include cleansing rituals, training programs, and special clothes. Among the Jewish people, the bar or bat mitzvah marks the transition of young men and women into adulthood. Less formally, acquiring a driver's license, getting a first job, and getting married are all rites of passage that indicate transition from one phase of life to another.

Humanistic and Utilitarian Ethics

Every individual in an organization has his or her own personal set of ethics. Personal ethics are a complex combination of experience, knowledge, and education. Moral philosophers outline two general threads of personal ethics, the humanistic and the utilitarian. In the humanistic tradition, there is an emphasis on the rights and importance of each person.

Humanism places a great value on personal freedom and responsibility. Utilitarian ethics, on the other hand, emphasizes the importance of choosing that action which will accomplish the most good for the most people. People who are guided by a utilitarian philosophy of ethics recognize that it is impossible to please everyone, but believe that the best course of action is that which pleases as many people as possible.

Ethical Behavior

One of the best ways to promote ethical behavior among employees is to offer direct training programs on ethical subjects. Often employees will make better decisions if they have considered and rehearsed their responses in advance. It is also important for an organization to have an explicit code of ethics for employee behavior.

Violations of the code should be punished, and noteworthy acts in accordance with the code should be rewarded. Sometimes, organizations find it useful to set up a system through which employees can report unethical behavior in the workplace. In many cases, employees who report such transgressions are guaranteed anonymity. Perhaps the best way to encourage ethical behavior is for management and supervisors to set a good example.

Organizations Social Responsibility

Organizations have a responsibility to conduct themselves ethically and in accord with the interests of the community. This responsibility supersedes the need to make profits. The first step in acting responsibility is to recognize the influence of the organization on the community in which it operates. In recent years, various ethical scandals have made the general public skeptical about the role of business in society. It is now more than ever important for organizations to act in the interest of the community, and to be sensitive to the desires of citizens. Indeed, the financial viability of a business is in part dependent on its reputation for social responsibility. In other words, working to promote the interests of the community can have a positive effect on the bottom line.

Consumer's Corporate Responsibility

Increasingly, consumers are aware of the effects of corporations on social and political life. Therefore, it is more important than ever for corporations to act responsibly and maintain a good reputation. There are a number of special interest and consumer groups that keep a close eye on corporate behavior, and are very willing to publicize transgressions. Ever since John F. Kennedy issued a Consumer Bill of Rights, normal citizens have felt empowered to investigate and criticize the behavior of corporations. Kennedy's Consumer Bill of Rights includes the rights to safety, to be heard, to choose, and to be informed.

Consumers' Right to Safety

One of the most fundamental consumer rights is the right to safety. The purchasers of a product or service should not run any risk to their health. To this end, manufacturers need to test products and provide clear and comprehensible instructions. In 1972, the federal government established the Consumer Product Safety Commission to monitor product safety. There are also a number of private organizations, most famously Consumer Reports, which evaluate new and existing products for safety. In addition, there are specific rules about product packaging, including rules that make it virtually impossible for products to be tampered with.

Consumers' Right to Be Informed

Part of the Consumer Bill of Rights is the right to obtain information about products and services. People should have the opportunity to learn as much as they need to before making a purchase. Perhaps the most famous example of this is the nutritional information published on food packaging; however, there are also important rules about how banks and utility companies disseminate information to the public. One of the federal departments charged with enforcing the provisions of the Consumer Bill of Rights is the Food and Drug Administration. In 1994, this department of the federal government issued labeling requirements related to nutrition. In 2004, the labeling requirements were expanded to include allergens.

Consumers' Right to Choose

One of the components of the Consumer Bill of Rights established during the Kennedy administration is the right to choose from a variety of products. No one business should be allowed to monopolize certain markets and the consumer should have a right to make selections based on price and quality. Of course, there are some cases in which it is not possible for there to be more than one provider in a particular market. For instance, it is not practical for there to be multiple water companies servicing a small town. In such a case, the federal government closely monitors the situation to ensure that the consumer is not exploited.

Consumers' Right to Be Heard

The Consumer Bill of Rights specifies that consumers have the right to voice their opinions about products and services. Consumers should feel free to make their opinions known to their communities and to the government. Businesses are encouraged to create customer relations departments, so that complaints and questions can be handled. In addition, many businesses now have detailed websites that allow consumers to respond. Not only does the right to be heard give consumers a say in their product choices, it also generates useful information about consumer preferences for businesses.

Corporate Responsibility to Employees

Corporations have a number of responsibilities to their employees besides fair compensation, equal opportunity, and safe work environment. Employees also have the right to be apprised of the company's fortunes, and to discuss professional issues with management. The Occupational Safety and Health Administration, established in 1970 by Congress are in charged with maintaining safe working conditions. It has over the past few decades established a wide-ranging set of standards for safety in all sorts of workplaces. Companies that fail to abide by OSHA regulations may be held liable.

Corporate Responsibility to Investors

When a corporation has investors, it has a responsibility to provide the best possible rate of return. Of course, not all investments will be profitable, but the corporation is responsible for doing its best to ensure success. When executives are overpaid or a corporation engages in insider trading, investors have a right to feel betrayed. Moreover, investors and potential investors have the right to access and evaluate corporate financial information. Investors have the right to be protected from the actions of people who have inside information. The Securities and Exchange Commission is responsible for investigating and prosecuting these rules related to insider trading.

Corporate Responsibility to the Environment

Corporations have a responsibility to avoid negatively impacting the natural environment. For a long time, American corporations were allowed to pollute the natural environment with impunity.

However, in 1970, the Clean Air Act established strict standards for automobile, plane, and factory emissions. This bill was amended in 1977 and 1990, and it now covers all motor vehicles. At the same time, two laws passed in the early 1970s forbid companies from contaminating water with pesticides and other chemicals. Legislation related to pollution of the land has taken a little bit longer. In 1984, the Resource Conservation and Recovery Act created rules related to the disposal of solid waste. By now, most corporations have found that it is both ethical and profitable to have a positive environmental impact.

Organizations Social Responsibility

Two of the most common ways for organizations to promote social responsibility are community support programs and social audits. There are all sorts of community support programs, from scholarships and school programs to charities and local infrastructure development. Many nonprofit organizations could not exist without major contributions by business.

A social audit, on the other hand, is a close and detailed look at the influence a business has on the community. By performing a social audit, a business can clearly determine how it is influencing its community, and how it can improve its relationship with the community members.

Caux Principles

Perhaps the most famous code of general business ethics was created at a meeting of top executives in Caux, Switzerland. This group, known as the Caux Roundtable, asserted two core principles: kyosei and human dignity. Together, these two concepts are known as the Caux Principles. Kyosei is a Japanese term meaning "cooperation for the common good." According to this concept, there is a place for competition, but not when it leads to diminished quality of life for others in the community. Proponents of kyosei believe that one firm's prosperity need not mean another's ruin. An emphasis on human dignity, meanwhile, entails treating other people as ends rather than means. In other words, businesses should treat others as they would like to be treated.

Egoism

Egoism is a system of ethics that emphasizes the promotion of personal interests. Egoists tend to believe that if everyone pursues his or her own interest, these interests will balance out.

Relativism

Relativism, on the other hand, is the belief that ethics change depending on the situation. What is ethical in one situation may be unethical in another.

Virtue Ethics

Virtue ethics, on the other hand, considers the established social mores to be a minimum standard of behavior and encourages people to go beyond these in their own conduct.

Kohlberg's Model of Cognitive Moral Development

The model of cognitive moral development advanced by Kohlberg outlines three categories of moral actors. Pre-conventional individuals base their behavior on rewards and punishments. Conventional people behave according to the values accepted by society. Finally, principled people adhere to their own moral code.

Sarbanes-Oxley Act

The Sarbanes-Oxley Act, passed by Congress in 2002, created tight regulations for accounting and reporting corporate financial information. This act came in the wake of several scandals that had diminished the confidence of investors. Corporate boards of directors were required to lower the number of directors directly employed by the corporation, and were required to publish specific statements related to financial reporting.

The punishment for violating these provisions could be very severe, including criminal charges as well as fines. Companies are required by the Sarbanes-Oxley Act to establish explicit ethical guidelines, create programs for whistleblowers, provide ethical training, reward compliance, and punish noncompliance

Fundamental Corporate Organizing Concepts

The structure of a corporation can be considered both vertically and horizontally. The vertical structure of a corporation is the hierarchy of command. The horizontal structure of a corporation is the division of specific functional departments, as for instance marketing, sales, and manufacturing. It is important for the employees and functional departments to be differentiated: that is, trained to perform specific tasks. However, it is also important for there to be good communication flow between the various functional departments in a corporation. Information should flow both vertically and horizontally. The ultimate responsibility for this flow of information lies with the executive staff and board of directors.

Compliance-Based Ethics Programs and Integrity-Based Ethics Programs

Two types of ethics programs used by corporations are compliance-based and integrity-based. Compliance-based programs establish clear codes of ethics, and then implement monitoring systems to ensure that employees are following the rules.

Ethics programs require the active participation of management, as well as the consistent enforcement of rewards and consequences. Any integrity-based ethics program, on the other hand, is more like an honor system. Each employee is asked to follow his or her own conscience and to be responsible for his or her own behavior. Integrity-based ethics programs also require the publication and dissemination of a clear and detailed code of ethics.

Social Responsibilities Corporation's Types

Types of social responsibilities corporations have are as follows:

- Economic responsibilities: the duties to provide quality goods or services at reasonable prices and to create the best possible rate of return for investors.
- Legal responsibility: the duty to obey local, state, federal, and international laws.
- Ethical responsibility: the duty to observe high standards of conduct, above and beyond what is mandated by law.
- Philanthropic responsibility: the duty to provide support and resources for charities and nonprofit organizations, as well as the responsibility to encourage employees to do the same.

Authority and Boards of Directors

In a business, authority is the ability and responsibility to make decisions. A person has formal authority when his or her position entails decision-making. For instance, in many small companies the owner has formal authority over all business decisions. Informal authority is derived from experience or expertise; an employee may obtain informal authority without ever being explicitly acknowledged by the organization.

In corporations, operations are managed by a board of directors, elected by shareholders. The members of the board of directors hire and fire executives, establish overall direction, review performance, and maintain high ethical standards. The members of the board of directors may be employees of the company, although they do not have to be.

CEO, Top Management Team, and Corporate Governance

The chief executive officer, or CEO, is the top executive in a corporation. He or she is only responsible to the owner and to the board of directors. Some companies combine the roles of president, CEO, and chairman of the board into one position. Sometimes, though, this leads to excessive power being concentrated in one person's hands, which can lead to mistakes. In recent years, it has become more common for chief executive officers to delegate their power to other top managers, as for instance the chief operating officer, chief financial officer, or chief information officer. Many organizations find that better decisions are made by a group of top executives, rather than by a single person.

Management Functions

Four Essential Management Functions

Four essential management functions are:

- *Planning*: the establishment of long-term goals and the specific objectives that must be reached on the way to these goals.
- *Organizing*: the creation of the departments and structures for the accomplishment of goals; a manager may need to hire specific employees in order to accomplish goals.
- *Leading*: promotion of positive thinking and morale in an organization; good managers are able to inspire and encourage their employees.
- *Controlling*: oversight and evaluation of professional performance; the establishment of rules and procedures for conduct and task performance

Basic Management Skills

Basic management skills consist of the following:

- *Planning skills*: outline and analysis of goals, charting of specific objectives, creation of schedules, assessment of resources, and identification of individual responsibilities
- *Decision-making skills*: assessments and evaluation of available options, followed by the making of well-considered choices
- *Meeting management skills*: selection of the right participants, development of agendas, efficient time management, and effective meeting guidance
- *Delegation skills*: effective distribution of tasks to those employees capable of performing them and comprehensive oversight of the delegated tasks

Performance Objectives

Established quality and time goals for the accomplishment of tasks are known as performance objectives. An effective manager establishes clear performance objectives so that employees will understand what is expected of them. Furthermore, it is a great idea to include employees in the creation of performance objectives. Employees, for instance, could be asked to create a first draft of the objectives, and then to modify the draft in consultation with the manager. This kind of system increases the employees' personal investment in performance objectives. In any case, performance objectives need to be directly related to job description. Employees should not be asked to perform tasks for which they have not been trained.

Major Management Theories

Major management theories include the following:

- *Classical management*: focus on increasing and maximizing productivity
- *Scientific management*: division of labor, standardization of tools, implementation of reward system, and emphasis on specialization
- *Classical organization theory*: emphasis on the design and maintenance of organizational structure; isolates the management functions of planning, organizing, leading, and controlling
- *Human relations approach*: emphasizes non-financial rewards for employees; focus on building morale and positive relationships

- *Behavioral science approach*: emphasis on improving productivity by minimizing office conflicts and maximizing employee motivation
- *Decision sciences*: focus on improving decision-making and eliciting employee participation
- *Systems theory*: emphasis on the examination of inputs, processing, output, and feedback, as well as the interrelations between these factors
- *Contingency theory*: focus on the differences between management situations, as well as the necessity of proper analysis

MAJOR CONTRIBUTORS TO MANAGEMENT THEORIES

Major contributors to management theories are:

- Frederick W. Taylor and Frank and Lillian Gilbreth contributed to scientific management by conducting studies of movement and time management
- Henri Fayol contributed to classical organization theory by outlining 14 principles of management and four basic management functions
- Elton Mayo contributed to human relations approach by focusing on social life and the flow of information within the workplace
- Mary Parker Follett contributed to the behavioral science approach by resolving conflicts and emphasizing consent of employees; subsequently, Hugo Munsterburg determined that efficiency is improved by care for employees
- Herbert Simon and James March contributed to decision sciences by drawing clear links between management and decision-making
- Chester Barnard contributed to systems theory by emphasizing the role of cooperation and inducements in organizations
- Joan Woodward contributed to contingency theory by discrediting the idea of a single effective management style and focused on the role of technology in organizational structure

MODERN MANAGEMENT THEORISTS

The following are modern management theorists and their theories:

- Peter Drucker focused on long-term business success and customer care. He also charted a path for continuing improvements and innovations within an organization
- W. Edwards Deming emphasized quality management and outlined 14 points of quality management, including training, leadership, and continuous organizational improvements
- Tom Peters listed nine components of effective companies, including trust in employees, organizational simplicity, flexibility, control of staff, and customer research
- William Ouchi created Theory Z, which combined the American focus on individual responsibility with the Japanese emphasis on group decision-making
- Michael Porter used economic reasoning to solve management problems and develop specific strategies for corporations
- Peter Senge emphasized the role of education in organizations, including a focus on systems thinking and mental models

SPAN OF CONTROL

The span of control in an organization is the number of employees who report directly to a particular manager. If the corporation has a narrow span, then there are many hierarchical levels, with each manager only receiving reports from a few employees.

Organizational Structure

In a corporation with a flatter organizational structure, managers will receive reports from a larger number of employees. Fine-tuning the span of control is important, because managers need to receive adequate information for decision-making without being overwhelmed. In the best scenario, employees are well-trained and capable of operating independently, but managers have enough information to make good decisions. In recent years, management experts have suggested that organizations with fewer layers tend to be more cost-effective. In response, many businesses in the United States have flattened out the organizational structure.

Review Video: Corporate Organizational Structure
Visit mometrix.com/academy and enter code: 752986

Delegation

Delegation is the distribution of responsibility and authority to subordinates. For instance, an upper manager might delegate the responsibility of running a meeting to a competent middle manager. Delegation occurs up and down the vertical hierarchy of an organization.

In order for delegation to be effective, the subordinate employee must understand and be capable of completing the delegated task. This means that the employee should have enough authority to make the decisions required for task completion. Once the delegated task is complete, the manager who delegated it should be capable of evaluating the report of the subordinate. In most organizations, final responsibility for a task lies with the manager who delegated it, rather than the subordinate who completed it.

Advantages of Delegation

When tasks are delegated, a manager has more time to devote to other, perhaps more important duties. Also, the subordinate who is assigned the task may improve his or her performance by gaining experience with new and more difficult tasks. Indeed, one way of determining whether employees deserve promotion is to evaluate their performance with delegated tasks. Research suggests that delegation can increase employee loyalty and innovation. Delegation can be viewed as a form of on-the-job training, which in the long run will empower employees.

Effective Delegation

Before a project can be effectively delegated, it must be defined in detail. The manager needs to be capable of fully explaining the task to the assigned employee. Also, the manager needs to be good at delegating tasks to those employees who are skilled and experienced enough to complete them. If there is any question about the employee's competence, the manager should be prepared to oversee the delegated task closely.

Oftentimes, it is a good idea to ask the opinion of the subordinate before delegating the task. When a task is delegated, a manager should ensure that the employee has sufficient resources and time to complete it. The subordinate employee may need access to special equipment or to other employees. Regardless, the manager should check with the subordinate frequently, to see if any problems or questions have arisen.

Decentralization in Organizations

In a centralized organization, almost all of the essential decisions are made by a core team of upper management. On the other hand, in a decentralized organization, much of the decision-making is delegated to subordinate employees. The appropriate structure for an organization depends on the level of knowledge and skill possessed by employees. If employees are capable of making decisions, then management would be wise to delegate decision-making and concentrate on other tasks. However, if employees are not especially knowledgeable, or if the interests of the various departments in the organization are in conflict, then important decisions should be made by senior management. Of course, many organizations successfully employ a mix of centralized and decentralized decision-making. Organizations tend to be less centralized when they are growing rapidly.

Managerial Decision-Making

In general, managers find that they make better decisions when they have access to more information. However, it is also important for a manager to bring creativity, experience, and knowledge to the process of decision-making. Managers often draw a distinction between tactical decisions, which relate to the short term, and strategic decisions, which relate to the longer term. A particular decision may be characterized by certainty, uncertainty, or risk. That is, the decision-maker may have all of the necessary information, little of the necessary information, or some information but no guarantee of success.

Intuitive Decision-Making

When a manager bases a decision on his or her beliefs or emotions, he or she is engaging in intuitive decision-making. Often, experienced managers make correct decisions without exactly knowing why. They just have a certain intuition derived from long interaction with a given set of variables. It can be difficult to make a case in support of such a decision; however, there are certain personality issues that can lead to poor intuitive decision-making. For instance, a manager might become overly convinced of his or her intuition, to the extent that he or she ignores obvious counterarguments. A manager might become addicted to making risky decisions. On the other hand, a manager might be afraid to make controversial decisions because of a fear of failure.

Systematic Decision-Making

A manager who weighs the various alternatives before coming to a decision is engaging in a systematic decision-making process. One of the prerequisites for systematic decision-making is access to all relevant information. A manager needs to be able to isolate the information directly related to the decision, and must have access to employees who know a lot about the subject. A manager must be able to evaluate both sides of the issue and obtain more information when necessary. The manager should be able to construct logical counterarguments for his or her final decision. Also, the manager should know when to draw on the expertise of colleagues.

Managerial Decision-Making Characteristics

One of the common characteristics of decisions made by managers is a lack of predetermined structure. In other words, managers are often called upon to solve problems without easy solutions. Many of the decisions made in an organization have preprogrammed answers, but managers are often required to create innovative solutions. For this reason, managerial decision-making entails a high degree of uncertainty. Managers are always at risk of making bad decisions. The best a manager can expect to do is minimize the amount of risk. A manager can expect to feel conflicted internally when making a difficult decision, and can expect negative feedback from others when making an unpopular decision

Rational Decision Model

In the rational decision model, the decision-maker uses all of the available data to select the most logical option. Of course, this is an idealized scenario; in real life, managers are always working with incomplete information. The rational decision model is most appropriate for programmed decisions and situations in which there is very little risk. Rational decision-making works better when decisions are made by a single person rather than a group. So long as the situation is predictable and all the advantages and disadvantages of various alternatives are clear, the rational decision model is the best.

Administrative Decision Model

Unlike other models of decision-making, the administrative model is more descriptive than prescriptive. According to the administrative model, perfect information is never available and no person is perfect at analysis. For this reason, decision-making is a process of inevitable risk. This decision-making model seems most appropriate for complex and uncertain decisions. It also seems to be a better descriptor of group decision-making than unitary executive decision-making. A manager is charged with making a satisfactory decision, not necessarily the best decision.

Political Decision Model

In the political decision model, the primary determinant is the anticipated reaction from those affected by the decision. The political decision model is most appropriate for decisions that need to create a consensus and minimize conflict. According to the political decision model, the best decision is not necessarily that which will achieve the best results. In political life, sometimes the best decision is impossible because of the attitudes of constituents. This decision model takes into account the necessity of popular support for some decisions. This model is considered most appropriate for situations with ambiguous information and large groups of stakeholders.

Decision-Making Process

Steps in the decision-making process are:

- The first step in the decision-making process is to identify the problem to be solved
- Next, a manager should make note of all the criteria related to the problem, as for instance the time, resources, and priority
- The manager should place these decision criteria in order
- Then, he or she can begin to generate options
- Once the list is complete, all of the available options should be surveyed objectively, with due attention to advantages and disadvantages
- After all of this information has been weighed, the manager should make the decision that creates the best possible outcome
- The decision will then be implemented, after which point the manager should receive feedback and evaluate the success of his or her decision

Factors Involved in Individual Decision-Making

Individual decision-making depends on a number of different factors. Some of these enhance decision-making, while others are obstacles to effective choices:

- *Individual values*: for instance, aesthetic, political, ethical, economic, or religious. Personality, gender, and social status: in some cases, a person's background can skew his or her perspective.
- *Risk tolerance*: the degree to which a manager can afford to make a risky decision. The assessment of risk will depend on the manager's evaluation of advantages and disadvantages.
- *Cognitive dissonance*: the difference between the situation as it is and the manager's perception of the situation. When there is a great degree of cognitive dissonance, decision-making tends to be poor.

DIFFERENT DECISION-MAKING STYLES

Just as managers all have different personalities, so do they have different decision-making styles. For instance, analytical decision-makers take a rational, measured approach. The focus of such a decision-maker is always obtaining as much information as possible.

A directive decision-maker, on the other hand, assembles important information but emphasizes the necessity of making a quick decision. A directive decision-maker is not afraid to take risk. A conceptual decision-maker tends to create a mental model of the situation, and then to base his or her decision on this model's predictions.

A behavioral decision-maker concentrates on the effects of the decisions of other people. This kind of decision-maker is likely to ask for the opinions of others before making a decision.

JUDGMENT ERRORS

Managers who become experienced at making decisions may develop some bad habits. For instance, managers often develop shortcuts, known as heuristics, which simplify the decision-making process. These are often helpful, but sometimes may lead to error. In the availability heuristic, for instance, a manager relies on his or her own memory rather than available information.

The representative heuristic, on the other hand, is the use of similar precedents to determine a decision, rather than attention to the facts as they are. Some decision-makers rely on an anchoring and adjustment model, in which obtained information becomes the foundation for future decision-making. Finally, some managers tend to stick by their decisions even when the evidence suggests they should do otherwise. This is known as the escalation of commitment to heuristic.

BARRIERS TO EFFECTIVE DECISION-MAKING

There a number of psychological biases that can negatively impact decision-making. For instance, some managers have an illusion of control, which leads them to believe they have influence over uncontrollable factors. If a manager is suffering from the solution, he or she will be unlikely to adequately assess risk.

Sometimes, a manager consistently makes bad decisions because he or she frames them incorrectly. In other words, the way information is presented can be as influential to decision-making as the content of the information. Some managers err by discounting the future, or overemphasizing short-term advantages at the expense of long-term factors. Finally, if a manager feels rushed, he or she is unlikely to make the best possible decision.

GROUP DECISION-MAKING

Group decision-making can be difficult, since a collection of people will bring their own prejudices and imperfect information to the problem. However, some situations call for the assembly of people with different areas of expertise. When a decision is not programmed (that is, when it does not have a ready solution), group decision-making tends to be less successful. Three ways to accelerate group decision-making are brainstorming, nominal group technique, and the Delphi technique. These are all methods of assembling and processing information as a group. One advantage of group decision-making is that it gives more people an investment in the ultimate success of the decision.

Possible Downsides

Possible downsides of group decision-making are:

- *Politics*: in some cases, the participants in a group will have different opinions and ideas about possible outcomes, and the ultimate decision may be made by a powerful coalition or by dominant personalities
- *Empowerment*: too many people can be asked to participate in the decision-making process, such that it becomes cluttered and overly complicated
- *Groupthink*: sometimes a group will tend in one direction at first, and group members will coalesce around this direction for fear of creating conflict
- *Corporate governance*: sometimes the rules of process within a corporation dictate the inclusion of certain unqualified members, which distorts the decision-making process

Brainstorming

Brainstorming as a group decision-making method; one way for a group to begin the process of decision-making is to brainstorm, or to generate as many ideas and possible solutions as possible, without attention to the likelihood of success. During a brainstorming session, there should not be any criticism, and group members should feel free to offer spontaneous suggestions. No contribution should be deemed unworthy of inclusion. Also, there should be no problem with ideas that conflict with those already given. At the end of the brainstorming session, all of the ideas can be compiled into a master list, at which point they can be considered more closely.

Delphi Technique

The Delphi technique is a method of making decisions that emphasizes reason and expertise. The first step is to send questionnaires to a set of experts in each particular field. So, for instance, a set of marketing-related questions would be sent to the top employees in the marketing department. The identities of these employees should remain unknown to the decision-makers.

These questionnaires should include a complete and detailed summary of the issues to be decided. There should be an opportunity for the recipients to ask questions and give feedback. Once all of the questionnaires have been returned, the staff members in charge of making the decision should compile and consider them.

NGT

In the nominal group technique (NGT)of decision-making, between seven and ten people are brought together for the sole purpose of making the decision. The group meeting is moderated by a facilitator, who introduces the members of the group, defines the issue, and lays out the instructions for decision-making. The participants in the nominal group should not be allowed to talk among themselves, a rule which is meant to discourage cliques.

After the issue has been introduced, the group will be given a set amount of time to brainstorm ideas, at the end of which each person will be asked to present his or her best idea. From this set of presented ideas, participants will create a list and vote. The results of the vote will be discussed, but the participants will not be encouraged to change their votes. Finally, the group will come to an ultimate decision.

MANAGE GROUP DECISION-MAKING EFFECTIVELY

Managing group decision-making traits effectively consist of:

- *Leadership style*: the leader of a decision-making group should prevent dominant personalities from overwhelming the discussion, should encourage participation by all members, should avoid groupthink, and should maintain the focus of the group throughout the process
- *Constructive conflict*: within any group making a decision, there is likely to be some conflict. It is important for a group leader to make sure that conflict is based on intellectual rather than emotional issues. The best way to promote constructive conflict is to maintain a tone of civility while exploring arguments and counterarguments
- *Enhancing creativity*: effective group decision-making should maximize the creativity of the group members, for instance, group members should be encouraged to brainstorm and improvise whenever possible. Also, group members should be encouraged to analyze feedback from customers where applicable

MANAGERIAL JOB OF PLANNING

In order for an organization to reach its long-term goals, a manager needs to produce specific plans of action. Plans must take account of the company's resources, both material and human, as well as the contours of the marketplace. When an organization engages in effective planning, it focuses on maximizing its advantages to meet the needs of the customer. However, an effective plan should take account of the current conditions without being excessively dictated by them. In larger organizations, it will be necessary for a manager to enlist the aid of many employees in order to construct a sufficiently detailed plan. Also, the manager will need to keep close watch on market conditions and business performance, so that plans can be modified as necessary.

SYSTEMATIC PLANNING

Systematic planning occurs at the corporate, business, and functional levels. Corporate-level planning is perhaps the most long-sighted: it involves the laying out of the organizational mission and objectives. This level of planning is also responsible for the distribution of resources within the various divisions and departments of the organization. Planning at the business level is focused on accomplishing the short- and long-term goals of specific divisions or departments. At this level, managers should have a better idea of the available resources, and should therefore be able to make more specific plans. Finally, at the functional level, managers are concerned with plans for the completion of specific projects. Functional-level plans tend to be restricted to relatively small periods of time.

ORGANIZATIONAL PLANNING

If an organization plans effectively, it can control the market instead of reacting to it. There are three current trends in business that underscore the importance of planning:

- *Cycle time reduction*: the cycle time is the length of time from the invention to the production of a good or service. In all industries, cycle times have been reduced, which means that organizations need to be better at anticipating their future actions
- *Organizational complexity*: the growth of successful companies and mergers between companies have resulted in a preponderance of large and complex organizations, such complicated organizations must be run with ever-increasing amounts of foresight
- *Global competition*: the improvement of communication and shipping technology has diminished the borders of business interaction. In order to meet the needs of a global marketplace, businesses must plan effectively

Benefits of Good Organizational Planning

The following are benefits of organizational planning:

- *Effort coordination*: an organization that plans well is able to harmonize the functions of various departments and divisions. The responsibility for coordinating plans lies with upper management.
- *Priority identification*: effective planning sets appropriate priorities and ensures that the most important tasks are performed first.
- *Definition of performance standards*: the criteria for performance quality are explicit and well-known, and managers ensure that employees are given tasks for which they are trained.
- *Management skill development*: managers actively seek out information and conflicting viewpoints, and are able to adjust their plans when necessary. Contingency and scenario analysis are two tools used by effective managers.

Scope, Timing, and Specificity in Organizational Plans

Scope: the set of business activities covered by a particular plan.

Time frame: the interval covered by the plan.

Level of detail: specificity of a plan; in the increasing level of specificity, plans can be corporate-level, business-level, and functional-level.

There is a great degree of variation in the scope, time frame, and specificity of corporate plans. The plans conceived by top management will have much less specificity than those imposed at a departmental level. However, the subsidiary plans created within specific departments must make sense as part of the overall plan. When the plan is given a specific deadline, this aspect of the plan often takes precedence over scope and detail.

Strategic, Tactical and Operational Planning

Strategic planning has to do with long-term goals, typically those to be accomplished over five or more years. For this reason, the strategic plan incorporates the company's mission statement; it has more to do with the long-term success and the identity of the business than with any specific targets.

Tactical planning, on the other hand, is typically aimed at goals to be accomplished over the next two to five years. Tactical plans may contain a number of options, each of which is believed to be appropriate for achieving the goals.

Operational planning relates to goals to be accomplished within the next two years. These plans are often very specific, including specific milestones and target numbers. An operational plan needs to take into account the available resources.

Corporate Planning Problems

Sometimes corporate planning goes awry. There are some common reasons for these problems. For instance, personal conflicts within the organization can lead to bad decisions, as can an inaccurate assessment of the organization's resources. Sometimes corporate plans are ineffective because a competitor unexpectedly emerges or launches a new product. More generally, a corporate plan may not be able to account for unpredictable and unforeseen changes in the industry or the marketplace. This is why it is a good idea for corporations to have long- and short-term plans. Long-term plans may need to be adjusted without necessitating changes to short-term policy.

Single-Use Versus Standing Plans

A single-use plan is one that is only likely to be used once. For instance, a business might need to develop a single-use plan for the creation and sale of a particular product. If the business is not going to be selling any other products, or any other similar products, the plan cannot be replicated in other areas of the business.

A standing plan, on the other hand, can be used again and again for similar functions. Standing plans are very useful for corporations, because they reduce the risk of individual error. Standing plans can be articulated as company policy, as specific techniques for the performance of common tasks, or as checklists to be followed by employees in the course of their work.

Strategic Map

A strategic map is a kind of chart on which an organization illustrates strategic, tactical, and operational goals. The strategic map should be easy enough for all members of the organization to read. On a basic strategic map, there are four drivers of long-term success: employee skills and opportunities for growth, effectiveness of internal processes, ability to provide value to customers, and ability to increase financial assets. On a comprehensive strategic map, each of these drivers will be represented and interrelated.

Planning Process

The first step in the planning process is to evaluate organizational status. For many companies, this entails competitive benchmarking or comparison with a top competitor. The business also might want to take stock of resources and assets. Next, the business establishes specific goals and determines the objectives that must be accomplished to reach these goals. Then, the business can develop plans of action, or specific ways to meet objectives. After this, the business can begin to distribute resources in order to execute the plans of action. The plan is then implemented. Finally, the organization evaluates and fine-tunes the implemented plan to ensure that the objectives are being met and progress is being made towards goals.

Business Success Objectives

Some objectives that are used to measure business success are:

- *Profitability objectives*: typically expressed as ratios, for instance the ratio of profits to capital (net worth), ratio of profits to total assets, or ratio of profits to sales
- *Marketing objectives*: often expressed as market share, available outlets, products in development, or sales volume
- *Productivity objectives*: typically expressed as a ratio of output to input, either as an entire organization or within a specific department
- *Physical and financial objectives*: quantity of accessible resources, both material and monetary
- *Quality objectives*: performance aspects related to the final physical product or service

Competitive Benchmarking

One of the ways that businesses assess their own performance and develop ideas for future progress is called competitive benchmarking. This entails close examination of the performance of another business, typically a top competitor in the same field. By analyzing the performance of the top competitor, a business can chart its own course for the future.

Common Liquidity

The common liquidity measures in business accounting are the current ratio, working capital turnover, accounts receivable, and the debt/equity ratio.

Ten Dimensions of Customer Service Quality

The ten dimensions of customer service quality are customer knowledge, competence, access, communication, courtesy, credibility, reliability, responsiveness, security, and tangibles.

Business Budgeting

Businesses use budgets when making plans and carrying out operations. A budget is essential to ensuring that a business does not plan activities that require more resources than the business can afford. All of the departments in a corporation should have separate budgets and administrative expense accounts. There should be an overarching budget system to coordinate the individual departmental budgets.

A financial budget incorporates financial statements, inventory budgets, and capital additions budgets to create a model of sales and expenses. Even when it is difficult to predict the market, a budget is necessary. The makers of a budget can allow for some variation by using moving budgeting, a technique in which the budget used for one time period is duplicated with necessary alterations. Another method of flexible budgeting is called variable budgeting: in this method, accountants explicitly allow for the possibility that profit may be different depending on changes in cost and productivity.

Quality Organization Values

When creating organizational plans, managers tend to keep in mind the same set of core values. These will include the values expressed in the organization's mission statement. Some of the most important values related to planning are performance standards and common features, that is, the common features of the product or service to be generated. A plan also needs to take into account the targeted reliability and durability of the products.

A manager will need to consider the aspects of the product that are most directly tied to customer satisfaction, especially when these are different from what the organization considers to be the most important characteristics. When making plans, a manager needs to take account of both internal environments (human and material resources and workspace) and external environments (legislation, market characteristics, and supplier cost and quality).

Methods for Implementing Plans

In some cases, a business implements plans on the sheer basis of its authority. When the plans are simple and the leadership of management is unquestioned, authority is a sound basis for the implementation of plans. However, in some cases a manager may need to use persuasion to implement a plan. This is especially true when a plan is complicated and controversial. Perhaps the best way to implement the plan is to encode it as a company policy. To be effective, a company policy should have the following characteristics:

- *Comprehensiveness*: capable of handling all possibilities
- *Coordination*: enables cooperation between departments
- *Flexibility*: allows for creativity and problem-solving by employees
- *Clarity*: clearly expresses objectives, proper techniques, and the scope of authority granted to employees
- *Ethics*: ethically correct and sensitive to cultural issues

Regulation and Standard Operating Procedure

Regulation is the basic set of prescriptions for the implementation of the policy.

Standard operating procedure is more informal than a regulation, an explicit set of guidelines for the benefit of confused employees.

Overview of Quality Planning

Quality planning: a useful practice both for internal processes and for the production of goods for the external market. W.E. Deming, a famed business consultant, asserted that quality planning is the process of identifying customer needs and selecting appropriate products and services to meet those needs. One particular system, known as total quality management, puts the focus on teamwork and organization-wide commitment to customer satisfaction.

PDCA Cycle

One of the most common quality planning cycles used in business is called the plan, do, check, act (PDCA) cycle. As the title indicates, the PDCA cycle has four steps.

- The organization identifies the quality improvement changes that need to be made
- The organization tests these changes with a small sample run
- the employees determine whether the implemented changes had the desired effect
- If the small sample run indicates that the changes were positive, the changes are implemented across the full range of production

Often, businesses will use the PDCA cycle in one production area to inspire changes in another

Time-Based Planning Concepts

The following are time-based concepts: concept-to-customer cycle, reengineering, the horizontal organization form, and CTR and its 3 percent rule.

- *Concept-to-customer cycle*: interval between the creation and sale of a product. In general, a fast concept-to-customer cycle leads to greater market share, customer satisfaction, and production quality
- *Reengineering*: any alteration to business processes that has the effect of improving service, price, quality, or efficiency. One example would be the purchase of new and better equipment
- *Horizontal organization form*: an organizational structure with fewer differences in status and authority. Reengineering often produces a more horizontal organizational form
- *CTR and the 3 percent rule*: cycle time reduction (CTR) is the business practice of streamlining production. Analysts assert that only 3% of an average processing period is spent actually doing the required work, for instance, a simple question from a customer may sit around for a long time before being answered

Negative Outcomes

When the firm does not pay enough attention to quality during the planning process, it may lose sales to competitors who deliver a higher quality product. In some cases, a manufacturer may be sued or held liable for a poor product. The company may ultimately need to throw away materials of inferior quality. In some cases, bad products can be a danger to the environment or to the public.

Revolutionary Planning Model

One quality planning model that helps to avoid these problems is called the revolutionary planning model. In this model, all the changes that must be made in business processes are performed at the same time. In the evolutionary planning model, on the other hand, a business makes changes incrementally over a long period.

Strategic Planning Process

The first step of the strategic planning process is to identify explicitly the purpose, mission, and values of the organization. Next, the planners need to determine goals and objectives for both the short and the long term. In doing this, the planners should identify the organization's core competencies and available resources, so that it can maximize their potential. Next, the planners should perform a detailed analysis of the business environment. After this, they can create a strategy for all departments and for the organization as a whole. The strategy should include performance expectations and target outcomes. The next step is to implement the plan and review the outcomes, for instance in terms of market share, product quality, and financial performance.

Mission Statement

A company's mission statement is an expression of its purpose, values, and goals. The mission statement should be general, but specific enough so that it can guide decisions in both the short and the long term. The mission statement should respect the history of the organization and the business environment in which the organization is operating. For businesses, a mission statement should have customer satisfaction as its focus. It should set achievable goals, and should provide inspiration for employees at all levels. It should indicate the specific areas in which the business wants to operate, so that the efforts of employees are not too diffuse.

SWOT Analysis

One simple tool for assessing the current health of a business is the SWOT analysis. SWOT stands for strengths, weaknesses, opportunities, and threats. The strengths of a business could be its resources, whether human or material. Experience and excellent training could be the strengths of a business. On the other hand, these same areas can be sources of weakness for a business.

A lack of expertise in the production area is a definite weakness. The opportunities of a business are the ways in which it could improve its position. The threats to a business are all of the potential problems, such as malfeasance or a general decline in customer demand.

Value Chain Analysis

A value chain analysis is a close look at the series of business activities that culminates in the delivery of a product or service. In a value chain, there are both primary and support activities.

- Primary activities include procurement, production, marketing, sales, and customer service
- Support activities include infrastructure development, research and development, and human resources

A business should analyze the costs and benefits of each of these activities. A value chain analysis will probably lead the organization to diminish the funds distributed to one activity and increase the funds targeted for another.

Corporate-Level Strategies

A strategy of single business concentration is a focus on one particular industry. Businesses that pursue this strategy have no problem related to dividing their resources, but they are susceptible to changes in a particular market. Businesses that are vertically integrated own multiple parts of the value chain. In other words, instead of paying other companies to assist in production, they handle operations themselves. Vertical integration is described as backward when the company owns the aspects of the supply chain before production. It is described as forward when the company controls the activities after production.

Diversification is a strategy of creating products for use in multiple industries. Diversification can be either related or unrelated, depending on whether the new industry is similar to the industries in which the business currently operates.

Portfolio Matrix Model

A portfolio matrix model of a corporation begins by identifying all of the departments and products of the business. Each of these components is known as a strategic business unit (SBU). These SBUs are placed in one of the following four categories, depending on their market growth rate and market share:

- Star: high share of a high-growth market; the high growth rate calls for significant financial backing.
- Cash cow: high share of low-growth market; will reward increased investment.
- Question mark: low share of high-growth market; should either be financed adequately or eliminated.
- Dog: low share of low-growth market; either barely self-sufficient or a drain on resources.

SBU Choices

Once a strategic business unit is designated as a star, cash cow, question mark, or dog, the portfolio matrix model recommends one of the following strategies:

- *Build*: devote more money to the SBU; a good choice for SBUs that are stars or have the potential to become stars.
- *Hold*: devote the same amount of money to the SBU; a good choice for maintaining the market share of cash cows.
- *Harvest*: extract as much immediate cash value as possible; a good idea when liquid assets are needed in other areas of the business; appropriate for all SBU types, with the exception of the star.
- *Divest*: remove financial support; appropriate for dogs.

It should be noted that SBUs can change type depending on their performance, changes in technology, and the market growth rate.

Business-Level Strategies

A business-level strategy aims at improving a company's competitive advantage. According to Michael Porter of Harvard, the most important determinants of profitability are rivalry between competitors, the relative bargaining power of suppliers and consumers, and the possibility of new and substitute products entering the market. Business-level strategies aim at improving product differentiation, customer focus, or cost leadership.

Product differentiation is the positioning of a good or service as being of better quality or somehow different from competition. In some cases, product differentiation causes lower volume and higher cost structure. If the company decides to focus on cost leadership, they will make every possible effort to reduce the price. The business will try to increase production volume and efficiency as much as possible. An integrated cost leadership/differentiation strategy tries to combine a unique product with low cost.

Functional-Level Strategies

Steps for accomplishing business-level strategies are functional-level strategies. Strategies at the functional level have to do with the procurement and distribution of resources, whether human or material. For instance, if a business takes a cost leadership approach at the business level, at the functional level it will make specific changes in materials purchased and equipment used. These changes will be aimed at improving efficiency and reducing cost. If the functional strategies are appropriate, they will be aligned with business-level strategies. Managers need to have a firm grasp of business-level strategy in order to select and implement appropriate functional-level strategies.

Strategic Planning Implementation Steps

There are four basic steps in the implementation of strategy:

- Strategic task definition: it is essential that the strategy be outlined clearly and in sufficient detail. The goal of the strategy must be the improvement of competitive advantage. The specific steps that need to be taken to improve competitive advantage must be listed.
- Organizational capabilities evolution: before the strategy is implemented, a group of knowledgeable employees, known as a task force, should be assembled to discuss the relative strengths and weaknesses of the organization with respect to the proposed strategy; the task force should report to upper management.
- Implementation agenda development: once the task force has reported, upper management will need to decide how the organizational structure should be altered to affect the new strategy; all of these changes should be published as a value statement.
- Implementation plan development: the construction of an implementation plan ensures that all employees understand their roles in the new strategy. The process should be monitored closely by upper management with advice and constructive criticism from members of the task force.

Internet and Strategic Planning

There are a number of reasons for businesses to use the Internet. For instance, many companies sell their goods online as well as through printed catalogs. These businesses use the Internet in a supportive role. For other businesses, however, the Internet is formative: that is, these businesses exist entirely because of the Internet. In order for a company to find success on the Internet, it must reach a large audience and must have sufficient content to attract attention. Many companies find it profitable to form affiliations with other firms on the Internet; these businesses link to one another, driving Internet traffic to their respective sites. For businesses that use the Internet in a supportive role, it is essential that online strategy be aligned with comprehensive business strategy.

Organizing and Organizational Structures

To organize a business successfully, there must be an appropriate structure for using the available resources to accomplish objectives. Each employee should have a reasonable scope of authority, and there should be enough hierarchy to ensure quality. In some cases, customer complaints about products or services are really about organizational structure. For instance, disagreements between two sections of the supply chain can result in a lack of quality in products. The interests of two departments may be at odds: for instance, the marketing department focuses on sales, while the manufacturing department may be more concerned with creating a quality product. It is the job of upper management to ensure that the various departments share objectives.

Fundamentals of Business Organization

Two fundamental concepts in business organization are differentiation and integration. When a business is differentiated, there are different departments, staffed by employees with different skills. The larger the business, the narrower the scope of each individual employee is likely to be. In very complex tasks, it is common for any large number of employees to contribute small portions. However, the efforts of all these employees must be integrated effectively. In particular, it is necessary for there to be efficient lines of communication between the various departments in an organization. It is the job of management to coordinate the efforts of highly specialized employees.

Organizations Integrate Differentiated Parts

The following integration methods help to ensure unity of effort by employees:

- Coordination by standardization and formalization: appropriate for stable work environments; employees are given directions and standard operating procedures, and are encouraged to interact through formal channels
- Coordination by plan: employees are given more leeway with respect to methods, but are encouraged to communicate with one another; appropriate when employees are very skilled
- Coordination by mutual adjustment: emphasis is on constant communication between departments; appropriate for simple tasks that require versatility
- Many organizations use combinations of these integration methods

Organizations Information Management

One way for organizations to manage information is to simply reduce the need for it. This can be done in part by establishing slack resources, which can be used in case material or personnel needs are underestimated. An organization often has part-time workers or extra inventory to serve as slack resources. Another way to reduce the need for information is to create self-contained tasks; that is, tasks which are performed in their entirety by one department. This reduces the need for inter-departmental communication. Another way to manage information is to improve the technology and structure of information sharing. Typically, this entails investments in computers and employee training. Often, businesses must spend the most time improving lateral communication: that is, communication between employees of similar status.

Responsive and Organic Structures Organizations

Some of the most responsive organizational structures are organic rather than bureaucratic or mechanistic. In an organic organizational structure, the responsibilities and scope of authority of an employee change depending on the tasks to be performed. Employees are given a great deal of autonomy, and are encouraged to ask one another for assistance. Information is available to anyone who requests it, and everyone has a good idea of who the experts are on each particular subject. This organizational structure has been found to improve employee commitment, and to inspire sound decision-making at all levels.

Organizing Core Competencies and Strategic Alliances

Some businesses place so much emphasis on their core competencies that they structure the entire organization around them. These organizations commit as much in the way of resources as they can to the improvement and maintenance of perceived advantages in technology, equipment, or human resources.

Another way to organize is around a strategic alliance. A strategic alliance is a formal relationship between two or more businesses, who have agreed to work together on mutual goals. These organizations may share ownership and management. Strategic alliances are a shortcut for businesses that want to quickly enter a market but are missing one key component. In order for a strategic alliance to prosper, both parties need to feel they are benefiting.

Learning Organizations

A learning organization prides itself on obtaining and disseminating information, and on being adaptable to changes in the marketplace. In such an organization, all decisions must be supported by empirical evidence, rather than the intuition of management. Learning organizations are typically very creative, but they pay close attention to their competitors. The flow of information through such an organization is very free, and is not limited to managers. Employees are constantly being pushed to improve themselves through education and professional development programs.

High-Involvement Organizations

In a high-involvement organization, on the other hand, employees are given a stake in the fortunes of the business. Managers will consult lower-level employees before making important decisions and employees will receive continuous feedback and progress reports from management.

CRM

One of the most important factors in the long-term success of a company is customer loyalty. Customer relationship management, or CRM, is a system for creating good communication with customers so that their needs can be met effectively. One of the foundations of customer relationship management is sophisticated technology for receiving and distributing information about customers. Companies should be constantly trying to improve their competitive advantage by improving quality and lowering price. Customer relationship management also focuses on internal customers: that is, the series of supply chain participants who successively add value to a product. In other words, customer satisfaction is no longer just the province of the marketing department.

TQM

The total quality management (TQM) approach emphasizes ongoing improvement of all processes. In order for the system to work, there have to be sophisticated systems for gathering information, measuring processes, and coordinating process improvements. The entire company needs to be in agreement in order for this approach to work.

Six Sigma Quality Approach

Another system of improving product quality is called the Six Sigma Quality approach. This approach is named after the Greek letter that defines the number of deviations in a process; when the sigma number is higher, there are fewer defects in a product or process. The Six Sigma Quality approach aims for 99.99966% instances of a product or process to be error-free. In so doing, they also hope to accelerate production cycles, improve customer satisfaction, and lower production costs.

ISO 9001 and Reengineering

The International Organization for Standardization (ISO) 9001 standards are appropriate for the improvement of the management system in any organization, and indeed they create improvements in quality for both producers and consumers. There are eight principles in this set of standards:

- Customer focus
- Leadership (communication of goals and vision)
- Employee involvement

- Process approach (identifying important tasks and assigning responsibilities for them)
- Systems approach to management (combining processes effectively)
- Continuous improvement
- Factual approach to decision-making
- Mutually beneficial supplier relationships

Around the world, more than 100,000 businesses have become certified according to ISO 9001 standards. Reengineering, meanwhile, is a process of revolutionary change in organizational systems. What is unique about this approach is that it is entirely based on customer desires. The company obtains information from customers and then reorganizes itself accordingly.

Technology and Organizational Agility

The organizational guru Joan Woodward has outlined three essential technologies for improving work processes:

1. small batch technologies, such as those used in job shops
2. large batch technologies, such as those used in mass production operations
3. continuous process technologies, which can be maintained at all times because they are performed by computers and machines

The high degree of mass customization in manufacturing these days has been made possible by complex networks of independent production modules. Each of these modules performs a different task, which is often controlled by computers. Another way that many companies are able to improve their flexibility and production speed is through lean manufacturing, in which production runs are short and scheduling is decentralized.

Some companies employ what are known as time-based competition strategies, as for instance logistics approaches, just-in-time operations, and simultaneous engineering. A logistics approach entails limiting transport to essential materials. Just-in-time operations create efficiencies by only producing necessary components and maintaining very small inventories. Simultaneous engineering coordinates all of the parts of the production process and requires the cooperation of suppliers and customers.

Craftsmanship Versus Scientific Management

Scientific management divides work tasks into small components, the performance of which can be measured and refined. One of the earliest proponents of this philosophy, Frederick Taylor, emphasized multistep processes and job specialization. He asserted that employees who perform the same simple task repetitively will become more efficient than employees who are responsible for a number of different tasks. The result is that many employees now have very little influence on planning and management, and instead perform the same rote task over and over again.

Craftsmanship, on the other hand, is marked by the presence of one employee on the project from its inception to its completion. In a craftsmanship model, managers are only there to handle resource needs and administrative issues. Employees who are allowed to be craftsmen tend to be happier, though their businesses may be less efficient.

Workplace Teams

Many businesses have developed workplace teams tasked with solving short-term problems, as well as teams that create long-term relationships between employees from different departments. In some cases, teams are coordinated and operated by managers, but in other cases the members of the team manage themselves. These self-managed teams can be a good opportunity for employees to develop new skills.

Quality Circles

A quality circle is a concept developed in Japan during the 1960s, which became popular in the United States for about fifteen years beginning in 1975: a group of less than ten people with roughly the same job description gather each week to discuss their work, and to come up with solutions to problems that have arisen. These groups often rotate the position of spokesperson, and this person voices their ideas and concerns to management.

Recruitment and Selection

Businesses use recruiting tactics to attract job applicants and manage their personnel needs. Large businesses need to plan hiring long in advance, so they hire special human resources employees to manage applications, interviews, and evaluations. The first step in the hiring process is a preliminary screening, during which candidates may be interviewed over the phone and resumes are reviewed. The next step is likely to be an in-person interview, which may be unstructured, semi-structured, or structured.

A semi-structured interview uses some standard questions, while a structured interview uses a standard set of questions for all applicants. Some businesses also administer aptitude, psychological, or personality tests. Next, a business will likely check the references of the remaining applicants, and may perform drug tests and background checks. Finally, candidates for management positions may be asked to participate in special leadership evaluations before hiring decisions are made.

Workplace Compensation

Employee compensation is usually thought of in monetary terms, as some compensation is not directly financial. For instance, vacation days, use of company resources and insurance are all forms of indirect financial compensation. Compensation is handled differently depending on the employee's position: some employees receive a flat rate for the amount of time they work, while other employees are paid based on what they produce. Some employees receive a combination of a flat rate and an incentive rate. Companies whose employees are members of a union typically receive a high flat rate established through collective bargaining.

When employees are paid according to individual incentive, they get a certain amount for each unit produced. A straight piecework wage consists of an hourly rate plus a little more for each unit produced. In a differential piece rate payment, the employer pays one rate for a low level of production, and a higher rate for greater production. In a production bonus system, the employee is given a flat rate payment and a bonus whenever their production is greater than a certain amount. Finally, a gain-sharing incentive plan gives employees a bonus when their group exceeds expectations.

Workplace Benefits

The United States mandates that companies pay unemployment insurance, Social Security, and workers' compensation benefits. However, companies may also pay for vacation days, other forms of insurance, child care, and employee pensions. A pension plan is meant to supply retirement income. Some companies opt to contribute to an individual retirement account or 401(k) rather than a pension plan. Also, many companies pledge to match the employee's contribution to the retirement or pension plan. In a cafeteria or flexible benefit plan, employees agreed to set aside a portion of their wage they will spend on things like insurance or child care. This money is not entered into yearly total wages and is therefore not taxed as income.

Workplace Training and Development

Companies receive a number of benefits from continuously training and improving the skills of their employees. Production and efficiency tend to go up, and businesses often discover that some employees are capable of taking on more responsibility, which leads to less money spent on oversight.

There's a slight distinction between training and development: training is learning how to perform a job for the first time, while development is learning how to perform an existing job better. Before training begins, employees are often given a needs assessment, so that their existing knowledge and skills can be assessed. Sometimes, performance on the needs assessment dictates the style of training. Businesses often provide basic orientation for new employees and diversity training so that employees harmoniously cooperate with colleagues from different cultures. For prospective managers, interpersonal training may be necessary. Some businesses have managers lead the training in what is known as coaching.

Profit-Sharing Plans

In a profit-sharing plan, employees receive an annual bonus if the business reaches a certain target of profit. The system tends to improve team spirit.

Merit Pay System, Executive Pay, and Pay Options

In a merit pay system, employees receive bonuses based on their individual performance. There must be a specific merit rating system agreed upon by managers. Around the world, there is a trend towards outsized executive salaries. For instance, in the past 30 years, CEO compensation in the United States has gone from 40 times to 500 times the pay of an average worker. This disparity is smaller in other English-speaking countries: British CEOs receive 130 times more than average employees, and Australian CEOs receive 50 times more. Increasingly, executives are paid in company stock and stock options rather than cash. A stock option gives the holder the choice of purchasing stock at a set price after a certain interval. When a business does well, stock options can be extremely valuable.

Work Team Roles and Strategies

One of the functions of a work place team is to allow team members to interact effectively with the external professional environment. For instance, many workplace teams have an assigned gatekeeper, who keeps the rest of the group abreast of advances in the profession. Three of the strategies used by teams to deal with external members are informing, parading, and probing. An informing team makes decisions internally, and then announces the decisions to others. A parading team focuses on building morale internally and projecting this strength outward. Finally, a probing team maintains steady interaction with customers, clients, and management and allows these relationships to guide external actions.

Lateral Role Relationships

Work-Flow Relationships

Work-flow relationships are based on the flow of material or information through a company; for instance, the employees responsible for calculating sales figures will have relationships with members of the accounting department.

Service Relationships

Service relationships are based on one employee's direct assistance of another, for instance, computer technicians provide services to accounts managers.

Advisory Relationships

Advisory relationships are based on the oversight of one employee by another, for example, a legal department oversees the operations of the sales team.

Audit Relationships

Audit relationships are based on the evaluation of one employee by another, for example, accountants monitor the financial activities of other departments.

Stabilization Relationships

Stabilization relationships are based on one department's need for permission from another department, for instance, sales departments may need permission from the accounting department to purchase advertising.

Liaison Relationships

Liaison relationships: based on a shared third party, for instance, many departments have direct contact with customers.

Organizational Structure

Organizational Design

Organizational design is the process of developing an organizational structure.

Mechanistic Model

Mechanistic model is a bureaucracy with central authority, rigid rules, and a great deal of specialization.

Organic Model

Organic model is an organizational structure with less emphasis on hierarchy, but more emphasis on versatility, in which employees are encouraged to innovate and are given a lot of autonomy.

Contingency Approach

Contingency approach is internal and external environment determines the design of the organization, for instance, advances in technology can spur alterations in organizational structure.

Multidivisional Organization

Multidivisional organization is a large organization composed of numerous, independent units, all of which share resources and information.

Network Organization

Network organization centers on changing relationships among manufacturers, consumers, buyers, and sellers. These organizations may be virtual, as when they only exist for a limited time, and modular, as when they consist of a central firm doing business with a number of peripheral organizations.

Job Analysis, Design, and Redesign

Job analysis precedes job design. The fundamental point of job analysis is to determine how a particular job meshes with the organization as a whole. The job analyst will make a list of all the activities associated with a particular job, as well as the skills required to perform it. From this summary will come an outline of job descriptions and job specifications. Job design is the conscious construction of a professional role, with the aim of increasing employee satisfaction and efficiency. During job design, the designer is focused on specialization, range, and depth. Job redesign is the refinement of an already-existing job. It may involve the use of flex time, rotation, enlargement, or enrichment.

Job Description

Job description: explicit verbal summary of the necessary skills, tasks, and equipment related to a job.

Job Specification

Job specification is a printed outline of the required knowledge and skills for a job.

Job Specialization

Job specialization is the degree to which an employee must perform different tasks; less-specialized jobs tend to have more range and depth. More specialized jobs tend to have less range and depth, and vice versa.

Job Range

Job range is the span of different tasks to be performed by the same employee.

Job Depth

Job depth: the latitude or autonomy granted to a particular employee.

Job Rotation

Job rotation is the movement of employees from position to position within an organization. Often, this strategy is employed to improve the skill base of each employee.

Job Enlargement

Job enlargement is an increase in the range of tasks performed by a single employee.

Job Enrichment

When employees feel that they do not have enough responsibility, are not growing professionally, and are not being recognized for their performance, they are more likely to perform below capacity or leave a job entirely. Job enrichment aims to reduce these occurrences by giving employees more autonomy and a broader set of skills. A job enrichment program can be expensive, however, so it is a good idea to determine whether an employee is willing before initiating one. An effective enrichment program will emphasize the following core areas:

- Skill variety: the employee is given a broader range of tasks to accomplish.
- Task identity: the employee is given charge of a task from its inception to its completion.
- Task significance: the employee is given more consequential tasks.
- Autonomy: the employee is given more freedom to pursue alternate methods.
- Feedback: the employee is given more response, both positive and negative, to his or her work.

Performance Evaluations

Performance evaluations may use graphic rating scales, ranking methods, or descriptive essays. They detail the strengths and weaknesses of an employee's work. Performance evaluations are used to determine employee placement, compensation, and training. Many managers use performance evaluations to motivate their employees, and this can be effective so long as the evaluations are perceived as fair. In a graphic rating scale, employee performance is assigned a rating from outstanding to poor. This descriptive method works best with small numbers of employees. Another way of expressing performance evaluations is with descriptive essays, but these are often hard to compare. It is easy for a manager's prejudice or particular judgments to skew an evaluation. For this reason, managers should be trained in the organization's particular methods. As much as possible, the performance evaluations should strive for specificity.

"Big Five" Personality Traits

The so-called "Big Five" personality traits related to work behavior are:

- Extraversion
- Emotional stability
- Openness to new experience
- Conscientiousness
- Agreeableness

Locus of Control, Internals and Externals

The extent to which an employee will take responsibility for himself or herself is tied to his or her locus of control, which is his or her perception of personal determination. An "internal" is a person who believes he or she has control, while an "external" is a person who believes he or she has little control. An external tends to need more supervision.

Type A and Type B Personalities

Employees can also be classified by whether they are Type A or Type B.

- A Type A personality feels the need to be superior to others, and tends to be aggressive
- A Type B, on the other hand, is more mellow and inclined to wait and see

Myers-Briggs Types

The Myers-Briggs personality classification system divides people into four cognitive styles: sensation-thinking, intuition-thinking, sensation-feeling, and intuition-feeling. The system also classifies people in terms of extroversion-introversion and a tendency towards judgment or perception.

Concepts of Perceptual Bias

Selective Perception

Selective perception is the conscious or unconscious removal of information that conflicts with a person's values or belief system.

Stereotyping

Stereotyping is an assumption about some other person based on his or her ethnicity, gender, religion, etc.; tends to cause misperceptions.

Priming

Priming: excessive emphasis on first impression.

Regency

Regency is excessive emphasis on the most recent impression.

Halo Effect

Halo effect is excessive emphasis on one trait of a person or situation; the selected trait may be positive or negative.

Attribution Theory

Attribution theory is concerned with the reasons for individual behavior. The behavior of some people is caused by internal circumstances, which are known as dispositional attributes. The behavior of other people may be the result of external circumstances, which are called situational attributes. One attribution theorist,

Harold Kelley, outlines the following three categories:

- Consensus: the degree to which people behave the same in a given situation
- Consistency: the degree to which a person's behavior is similar in different situations
- Distinctiveness: the degree to which a person's behavior changes in different situations

There are also a number of attribution biases, such as an overemphasis on personality traits. Also, in some groups there is a tendency to overestimate the degree to which the parties agree a phenomenon known as false consensus. Sometimes the members of a group overestimate the positive effects of their own personality, in what is known as the self-serving bias.

Job Satisfaction and Attitude

An attitude is a belief that has been reinforced by experience and longevity. Although attitudes are typically well entrenched, they can change. Job satisfaction is one such attitude. Though it can be difficult to improve, management surveys have shown positive results with better supervision, decentralization of decision-making, improved pay, and more attention to the match between the employee and the task. Organizational commitment is another major determinant of job satisfaction. There are three types:

- *Affective commitment*: emotional affiliation with the goals, values, and mission of the organization.
- *Normative commitment*: feeling of loyalty to the other members of the organization.
- *Continuance commitment*: the tendency to stay with an organization rather than risk failure elsewhere.

Douglas McGregor's Motivational Theories

According to Douglas McGregor, there are two possible explanations for workplace behavior, known as Theory X and Theory Y. Theory X assumes that workers require direction from management, and that their behavior can be pinned to persuasion, punishment, rewards, and coercion. According to Theory Y, employees want to succeed, but will not thrive unless they are given autonomy. This theory suggests that employees should be given opportunities to increase their participation. According to McGregor, the intrinsic rewards of the job are the psychological benefits the worker obtains from accomplishing his or her tasks well. The extrinsic rewards, on the other hand, are the payments and benefits given by the employer.

Goal-Setting Theory

Goal-setting theory is concerned with the forces that inspire employees to work towards organizational goals. Theorists have discovered that the most effective goals are those that have meaning for the employees, either by aligning with their personal values or with their belief systems.

An appropriate goal is a challenge but is not so difficult as to be overwhelming. This sort of appropriate goal is known as a stretch goal, because it forces the employee to improve his or her skill set and performance.

There is also some stretching within the organization itself. An organization can stretch vertically, as when productivity is increased, or horizontally, as when employees improve their skills and become autonomous in new tasks. It is essential for goals to be aligned with the skills of the employees. When team performance is the most important variable, teamwork should be the center of goals

Maslow's Hierarchy of Needs Theory

According to Abraham Maslow's hierarchy of needs theory, the requirements of a human being can be separated into different categories by their importance. Maslow asserted that one way to meet these needs is through work. If a particular need is not being met, it will create an internal tension that may lead to problematic behavior. The needs are listed below in order of ascending importance:

- Physiological needs, such as food and sleep.
- Safety needs, such as security and shelter.
- Social needs, such as love and friendship.
- Self-esteem needs, such as respect and good reputation.
- Self-actualization needs, such as personal growth and development.
- The lower-order needs often supersede the higher-order needs, a phenomenon Maslow called prepotency.

Clayton Alderfer's ERG Theory

One off-shoot of Maslow's hierarchy of needs theory is Alderfer's ERG theory, in which there are only three primary needs:

- *Existence*: most important needs for survival; for example, food and shelter
- *Relatedness*: need for connection to other people, for instance, the needs for love and friendship
- *Growth*: the needs for improved knowledge and the need for innovation

According to Alderfer, humans can begin to satisfy higher needs only after lower needs have been met. However, the failure to satisfy a higher need may result in a return to preoccupation with lower needs, a phenomenon Alderfer called frustration regression. An example of this is when people seek comfort in food after suffering an interpersonal setback.

David McClelland's Learned Needs Theory

According to the learned needs theory advanced by David McClelland, the best motivation is a personal history of accomplishment. One of McClelland's most famous techniques was to present a person with illustrations or photographs and have them write an accompanying story. In cooperation with John Atkinson, McClelland developed a way to score the Thematic Apperception Test (TAT) created by H.A. Murray. The intention was to develop a method for determining a person's desire for achievement and power.

McClelland identified three dominant needs: achievement, affiliation, and power. The extent to which one of these needs predominates in a single person suggests the appropriate line of work for that person. People with a strong need for affiliation are best suited for work in a team, while people with a great need for power are better suited for positions of authority.

Frederick Herzberg's Two-Factor Theory

Frederick Herzberg performed an extensive study of accountants and engineers and came to the conclusion that no one characteristic of a job is entirely responsible for satisfaction. On the contrary, job satisfaction is based on hygiene factors and motivator factors. Hygiene factors are peripheral to the job itself, and include the following:

- Workplace physical environment
- Employee pay, job security, and status
- Relationships with superiors
- Technical supervision by management
- Organizational policy and procedures
- Motivator factors, on the other hand, are intrinsic to the job, and include:
- The actual task to be performed
- Responsibility for actions
- Potential for personal growth and education
- Recognition from superiors
- Advancement within the organization
- Achievement

Process Theories of Motivation

According to process theories of motivation, a person's internal drive is the result of mental decisions and intentional thought processes. The two main branches of process theory are expectancy theory and equity theory.

Expectancy theory, which is also called VIE (valence, instrumentality, expectancy) theory, outlines motivation as a product of the perceived effort required to accomplish something and the perceived desirability of that accomplishment. In other words, a person is more likely to do a job if they believe their work will be rewarded and that the reward will be worth the work. The link between work and reward is called instrumentality.

Equity theory, on the other hand, emphasizes perceptions of fairness and justice in the workplace. Employees tend to work hard if they feel that others are working hard, and that their own efforts are being justly rewarded. The ratio of individual effort to reward is called the reference ratio. Perhaps the most famous proponent of equity theory was J. Stacy Adams.

Two Environmental Theories of Motivation

The environmental theories of motivation focus on the ways in which behavior is learned over time. The two main branches of environmental motivation theory are reinforcement theory and social learning. Among reinforcement theorists, of whom the most famous is probably B. F. Skinner, motivation is believed to be dependent on the consequences of similar actions in the past. Reward may be defined as contingent, if it has to do with the specific behavior, or non-contingent when it does not seem tied to behavior. Managers can use positive reinforcement (contingent rewards) or negative reinforcement (removal of negative consequences) to motivate behavior.

Bad behavior, on the other hand, can be minimized with punishment or extinction (no response). Social learning theory, as advanced by Albert Bandura, emphasizes the importance of role models in the development of good behavior. Specifically, Bandura pointed to attention, retention, reproduction, and motivation as the steps of the social learning process.

Managing Rewards and Punishments

In order to be consistent and effective, managers need to define the behaviors to be reinforced, rewarded, punished, and extinguished. All too often, a manager reinforces bad behavior by failing to identify successful deeds that were accomplished in the wrong way. The reinforcements should be appropriate to the individual employee. Money is not the only reinforcement in the workplace: managers can also use increased autonomy, personal recognition, and benefits to reward employee performance.

Of course, managers and employees will inevitably make mistakes. If these mistakes are made in good faith, punishment should not be severe. Nevertheless, managers should implement disincentives and ensure that mistakes are dealt with constructively. The best way to run a reinforcement and punishment program is with consistent, detailed feedback.

Hackman and Oldham Model

According to the researchers Hackman and Oldham, employees are motivated, satisfied, and productive when they are given meaningful work and adequate feedback. The most positive employee psychology is associated with:

- *Skill variety*: a wide range of tasks, requiring different levels of skill, knowledge, and concentration.
- *Task identity*: participation in all phases of a project's completion, from conception to production.
- *Task significance*: the investiture of work with personal and social meaning, in other words, the feeling that one's work is important and beneficial.
- *Autonomy*: independence and freedom in the selection of methods and strategies.
- *Feedback*: consistent praise and constructive criticism about performed tasks.

Job enrichment programs are successful in proportion to the employee's desire for self-improvement.

Empowerment in the Workplace

In the workplace, employees are empowered when managers discuss decisions and allow employees to give input. Empowered employees feel better about their performance, and tend to make a more personal investment in their tasks. For this reason, they are more productive and effective. In order for employees to be empowered, they must be given a great deal of information and autonomy. When they make good decisions, they should be rewarded. One of the benefits of empowering employees is that it reduces the responsibility for supervision by managers. Of course, in the early stages of empowerment, the managers must maintain good oversight and give clear directions. Also, when empowered employees are given tasks to perform outside their usual job description, managers should provide close supervision.

Leadership

Leadership is the development of an organizational vision, as well as the day-to-day guidance that encourages the team to work toward that vision. In business, a leader's vision is likely to include financial return for investors, quality products or services for customers, and efficient work within the organization. The theorists James Kouzes and Barry Posner outlined five important behaviors in a leader:

- Leaders question conventional beliefs and techniques
- Leaders inspire others to a collective vision
- Leaders provide their subordinates with information and autonomy
- Leaders model the organizational vision in their own behavior
- Leaders reward and appreciate their subordinates

Leading and Managing

Leadership and management are similar, though management tends to be concerned with daily operations, while leadership has more to do with overall vision. Leaders establish the general direction of the organization, while managers create plans and budgets. Of course, the leader and the manager may be the same person. Nevertheless, a person in a leadership role needs to take a long-term, detached perspective.

A manager, on the other hand, has to engage with the details of operations. Leadership can be described as supervisory or strategic. Supervisory leadership entails daily direction, support, and feedback. Strategic leadership, on the other hand, is more concerned with creating a climate of motivation and optimism within a company.

Leaders and Followers

Managers have to be both leaders and followers, insofar as they direct the actions of subordinates and report to upper managers or executives. Some of the characteristics that make a good follower are also those that make a good leader. Both leaders and followers need to understand their job tasks, have some autonomy, and understand their position in the organization.

Leaders are successful when their followers can manage themselves and enhance their own importance. In order for followers to improve themselves, they need feedback and training by managers. Performance evaluations are a good venue for this sort of improvement. Over time, leaders and followers will learn better how to deal with one another to create positive change.

Power That Leaders Can Use

Legitimate Power

Legitimate power is the authority of a manager to issue commands to subordinates. In most organizations, the legitimate power of a manager is limited, so that he or she is only responsible for a defined range of employees and tasks.

Reward Power

Reward power is the authority of a manager to offer and distribute incentives, such as raises and bonuses.

Coercive Power

Coercive power is the authority of a manager to discipline and punish subordinates.

Referent Power

Referent power is the authority of a manager that derives from his or her charisma, style, and other personal qualities.

Expert Power

Expert power is the authority of managers that derives from his or her exceptional training or knowledge of a certain subject.

Trait Theory of Leadership

According to the trait theory of leadership, all successful leaders have certain personal characteristics in common: initiative, ambition; energy, desire for improvement, self-assurance, competence, and a firm grasp of the strengths and weaknesses of others.

Stogdill's Handbook of Leadership identifies the following traits common to good leaders:

- *Capacity*: knowledge, intelligence, focus, creativity, and judgment
- *Achievement*: accomplishments and education
- *Responsibility*: persistence, reliability, and determination
- *Participation*: cooperation, friendliness, helpfulness, and selflessness
- *Status*: popularity, reputation, and deference from colleagues

One criticism of this leadership theory is that it places all the emphasis on the leader, ignoring the employee, and it fails to differentiate between traits.

Behavioral Theory of Leadership

The behavioral theory of leadership, which began with the early work of Rensis Likert and his colleagues at the University of Michigan who identified job-centered and employee-centered leader behaviors. There are two leadership behaviors at the center of the behavioral theory of leadership: task accomplishment and sensitivity for the feelings of subordinates. A leader who demonstrates both of these behaviors will always be effective. In the work of Likert and his associates, there was special attention to three leadership behaviors:

- *Task performance behavior*: related to specific processes and performance of work tasks
- *Group maintenance behavior*: teambuilding and supportive leadership
- *Decision-making*: may be either autocratic or democratic

An autocratic decision-making style may result in higher performance, but the democratic style seems to result in happier employees. Leaders who make no decisions (that is, leaders who have adopted a laissez-faire style) create low performance and low employee satisfaction. Leaders who pay great attention to maintenance behavior tend to retain their employees far longer.

Situational or Contingent Leadership Theories

According to contingent (also known as situational) leadership theorists, the most effective strategy for leading a group depends on the circumstances. In other words, there is no one set of leadership skills that works in every case. Situational leadership centers around three approaches:

- The first approach emphasizes harmony between manager and situation
- The second approach emphasizes the probability that a manager will have to modify his or her approach in a given situation
- The third approach centers on the way some situations can mitigate or neutralize the skills and style of the leader

At this point, most leadership theorists believe that the second approach is the most consistent with reality.

Situational Factors

In order to make the proper decision in a given situation, a leader must be able to analyze three crucial elements: the manager, the subordinate, and the situation.

- *The manager*: beliefs, management style, degree of trust in employees
- *The subordinate*: training, expertise, and capacity to make important decisions and assume autonomy, and the degree to which he or she subscribes to the goals of the organization
- *The situation*: style of leadership approved by the organization, harmony within the group, sufficiency of resources, and available time

It will also be necessary for the manager to account for his or her level of expertise, the significance of the decision, and the amount of time allowed for the decision.

Vroom Model of Leadership

The Vroom model of leadership is based on a situational assessment matrix in which five decision-making styles (consult individuals, consult the group, decide, delegate, and facilitate) are placed along the y-axis and problem analysis factors are placed along the x-axis. The Vroom model generates a recommended leadership style given the circumstances.

Fiedler's Contingency Model

The contingency model of leadership effectiveness advanced by Fiedler generates recommendations with a chart taking into account task structure, the position power of the leader, and the health of relations between leaders and employees. The recommended leadership style may be task-motivated or relationship-motivated. Fiedler assessed leadership by taking a look at the relationship between the leader and his or her least-preferred coworker (LPC). A task-oriented leader will criticize the LPC's work, while a people-oriented leader will simply avoid the LPC.

Hersey-Blanchard Situational Leadership Theory

According to the situational leadership theory advanced by Hersey and Blanchard, leaders must adjust their behavior depending on the circumstances in which they find themselves. The Hersey-Blanchard situational leadership chart places task behavior on the horizontal axis and relationship behavior on the vertical axis. The appropriate leadership style depends on the willingness, ability, and confidence of those who will be following the order.

- *Telling*: leader gives detailed instructions and oversees performance closely, appropriate when the follower is unsure or unwilling
- *Selling*: leader gives reasons for his or her decisions, and allows the follower to ask questions and receive clarification, appropriate when the follower is willing but inexperienced
- *Participating*: leader collaborates on ideas and guides decisions, appropriate when followers are capable but unmotivated
- *Delegating*: leader delegates authority and responsibility to subordinates, appropriate when followers are capable, committed, and confident

The Hersey-Blanchard model emphasizes both professional and psychological maturity.

Path-Goal Theory of Leadership

The path-goal theory of leadership advanced by Robert House and Terrence Mitchell defines the leader as the link between the organization and the employee. If the leader is successful, there are positive outcomes for both parties. There are four productive sorts of leadership behavior:

- *Directive behavior*: goals are established, work flow is organized, and feedback is offered frequently, appropriate when close supervision is necessary.
- *Supportive behavior*: special attention to the thoughts and decisions of the employee, appropriate for especially challenging situations.
- *Participative behavior*: delegation of some authority to employees, appropriate when employees are motivated and competent.
- *Achievement behavior*: goals are lofty but realistic, appropriate when employees are competent but perhaps unmotivated.

House and Mitchell also outlined some important environmental and subordinate situational factors, like authority structure, experience, and ability.

Neutralizers and Substitutes for Leadership

In some workplaces, the traditional approaches to leadership are not feasible. Aspects of the work environment may neutralize or substitute for leadership. A situation is described as a neutralizer when it keeps the leader from changing the behavior of employees. For example, there may be a corporate contract with all employees that prevents the manager from giving bonuses or raises to top-performing employees.

In other situations, factors may substitute for leadership. The best examples of leadership substitutes are training and education. However, some tasks are themselves so rewarding and educative that leadership is unnecessary.

LMX Theory

The leader-member exchange (LMX) theory analyzes leadership as a set of relationships between leader and individual followers. In these relationships, roles must be negotiated. A leader will have varying degrees of influence and success in modifying the behavior of different employees. If the leader and employee have a low-exchange relationship, the employee receives basic rewards for following a clear set of rules.

If the relationship between the leader and the employee is high exchange, on the other hand, the leader has the power to give the employee special rewards. Because the leader has different relationships with his or her employees, there is a tendency for in-groups and out-groups to develop. The in-group is the set of people closest to the leader. One problem with this scenario is that the leader will have a tendency to discount the achievements of those in the out-group and overvalue the contributions of those in the in-group.

Leadership Types

Group Maintenance Behaviors

Group maintenance behaviors promote group harmony and satisfaction.

Charismatic Leadership

Charismatic leadership derives its power from the positive, magnetic personality of the leader.

Transformational Leadership

Transformational leadership is successful when the members of a group move past their own concerns and act in the best interests of the group.

Transactional Leadership

Transactional leadership participation and success are motivated through a system of rewards and punishments.

Level 5 Leadership

Level 5 leadership is a combination of transactional and transformational leadership with an emphasis on personal accountability and persistence.

Authentic Leadership

Authentic leadership is based on the perceived honesty and integrity of the leader.

Servant-Leader

Servant-leader is when employees are treated in the same way as are customers of the organization.

Bridge Leaders

Bridge leaders are people who inhabit two roles or communities, and work to connect them.

Shared Leadership

Shared leadership is when authority shifts depending on the task being performed.

Lateral Leadership

Lateral leadership is when a group of employees with the same status cooperate on a project.

Emotional Intelligence and Self-Leadership

To be effective, a leader must have experience, intellectual capacity, and emotional intelligence. Emotional intelligence consists of characteristics such as motivation, empathy, social skill, self-regulation, and self-awareness. The trend in the United States towards less middle management has forced lower-level employees to be more autonomous. For this to work, employees must be given better opportunities to develop and learn. In the management philosophy of self-leadership, employees are encouraged to align their personal agendas with the goals of the organization at large. The leader is less a commander than a role model for subordinate employees. The following are components of self-leadership:

- *Self-set goals*: that is, set by the employees
- *Self-observation*: system of evaluation and record-keeping by the people performing the task
- *Self-rewards*: positive reinforcement delivered by the employees themselves
- *Self-cueing*: rehearsal or planning of an activity by the employees who will be performing it
- *Self-designed jobs*: proposed or planned changes made by employees

Cognitive Self-Management

Cognitive self-management strategies include the generation of positive mental images related to professional success. Two of these strategies are:

- *Opportunity building*: creation of new venues through which an organization can achieve success
- *Positive self-talk*: generation of self-esteem-building images and thoughts; the conscious visualization of success has been shown to contribute to actual success

Development of a Self-Leadership Culture

The creation of an effective self-leadership culture requires the laying of significant groundwork:

- *Sharing information*: in order to work independently, employees need sufficient information; there cannot be any secrets kept by management if employees are to have the full range of tools and resources available
- *Training*: in particular, employees need to be trained to handle difficult situations independently, and the training program should be aligned with managerial policy
- *Reinforcement*: employees should be rewarded for success

Management Control Overview

Consideration of the control process is relevant to all businesses, not just manufacturers. Everyone should take an interest in the manner by which products are created and distributed. The emphasis of management control can be on a number of different things: means control; variances and errors; employee and customer attitudes; or operational productivity, just to name a few.

In the control process, one such variable is compared to targets. Special attention is paid to three elements of the control process:

- Specification: the desired technical characteristics of the product or service, which must be expressed in detail and with verifiable measurements
- Production: the tasks that must be performed to meet the task objectives. Operational measures provide the basis for evaluating the success of tasks and of the final product
- Inspection: assessment of whether a product or task meets specifications. In large-scale production, it is common for firms to use statistical sampling techniques and to make specific technical corrections when there are significant deviations

Preliminary Control Measures

The aim of preliminary control measures is to prevent deviations related to the quality and quantity of resources. There must be adequate material and enough competent employees to accomplish the organization's goals. The following areas require the most attention with regard to preliminary control:

- *Human resources*: hiring people who can become competent and autonomous
- *Materials*: use of statistical sampling to ensure that raw materials conform to standards of quality, to ensure that delivery is on time, and to ensure that inventory is appropriate
- *Capital*: a strict budget should be maintained, and only those activities which will lead to profit should be funded
- *Financial resources*: sufficient for interest payments, materials, and wages; should take into consideration the operating cycle, inventory level, necessity of cash, and variability in the cost of materials

Preliminary Control of Capital

Capital budget documents are a good way for capital acquisition managers to predict how investments and purchases will turn out. The intention of capital acquisitions is to improve quality, productivity, customer service, and capacity. The most popular capital control methods are:

- *Payback method*: rather than considering profitability or the time value of money, this is a calculation of the interval needed to repay capital acquisitions out of future cash earnings
- *Rate of return on investment*: ratio of extra net income to original investment; this method takes account of profitability but not the time value of money
- *Discounted rate of return*: similar to the payback method, with added consideration of cash outflow and inflow

In each of these methods, the acquisition manager compares the planned purchase to a known standard

Concurrent Control

Concurrent control is a philosophy of constantly monitoring operations to ensure that they are in line with explicit company policy. Supervision is one of the tools of concurrent control, although it must be preceded by effective and comprehensive direction. The amount of direction needed before tasks begin depends on their difficulty and the competency of the employee receiving direction.

Managers at all levels are responsible for directing employees although the most direct instruction will come from first-line supervisors. Without sufficient information, employees cannot be expected to accomplish their goals. Nevertheless, the manager needs to understand that employees can easily be overwhelmed by too much information, especially when much of it is irrelevant.

Financial Statement Analyses

Managers use financial statements to evaluate trends. For instance, an organization's balance sheet suggests its current financial status, while its income statement describes its performance over a specified interval. When determining whether they have the assets to meet their current obligations, managers use liquidity measures like the current ratio, which is the ratio of current assets to current liabilities, and the acid-test ratio, which is the same as the current ratio except it omits inventories and prepaid expenses.

Assets are defined by looking at the accounts receivable turnover, which is the ratio of credit sales to average accounts receivable, or the inventory turnover, which is the ratio of the cost of goods sold to average inventory. If the inventory turnover is high, there may not be enough for upcoming sales. Managers must also take a look at solvency measures, which indicate the firm's ability to meet its long-term obligations. The most important of these is the ratio of net income before interest and taxes to interest expense. The company's financing can be measured via a debt/equity ratio or debt/asset ratio.

Standard Cost Analysis

In standard cost analysis, managers compare actual costs with the normal level of costs. This is a good way to tell when organizational purchases are running too high. One of the newest forms of cost accounting, called activity-based accounting, focuses on the activities that consume resources. Accountants consider the amount of time spent by each employee on a given activity, and assign this time a financial value. The actual cost of a product, then, is not only the cost of the materials, but also the cost of the time spent creating it.

SPC

Statistical process control is a system of minimizing variability and errors in production systems. SPC, as it is known, requires observation and representation in pictorial charts and diagrams. This system requires a mixture of descriptive and inferential statistics. Inferential statistics compare several sets of data in the hopes of identifying problematic production processes. There will always be some variation in processes, but SPC aims to minimize it. This system differentiates between random (common cause) variation, which can be reduced almost, but not quite, to zero, and nonrandom (special cause) variation, which may be totally eradicable.

Quality Control Tools

Flow Charts

Flow charts processes are depicted as inputs, outputs, processing; there is also space for potential changes to the process.

Run Charts

Run charts depict the changes and problems that affect an organization over a particular interval; it is a two-axis chart, in which the horizontal axis is time and the vertical axis is quality.

Control Charts

Control charts illustrates the degree to which a process is managed closely, i.e., the degree to which variations and deviations are avoided.

Fishbone Diagrams

Fishbone diagrams illustrate the causes and consequences of a problem.

Pareto Charts

Pareto charts illustrate the number of product or service defects over time, and aims to eliminate the most trouble with the least possible effort.

Histograms

Histograms indicate the repetition of certain numbers in a series of measurements and it is used to assess the variability of a product.

Scatter Diagrams

Scatter diagrams displays the relationships between two variables, such as the relationship between materials and product quality.

TQC

Total quality control (TQC) is a system for maintaining sufficient quality to keep customers satisfied. This phrase was most likely created by Armand Feigenbaum. Instead of putting the last person on the production line in charge of assessing total quality, the TQC system spreads responsibility out along the entire chain.

In this model, every successive participant in the production chain is seen as creating a product for the next person, whether that person is the customer or another employee. The TQC model is often augmented with statistical process control (SPC) techniques. However, many managers feel that

TQC is better at adapting to a changing marketplace. This system minimizes quality problems through:

- Initial quality guidelines
- Training in quality
- Quality control in design, procurement, processing, testing, and inspection
- Control of non-conforming material
- Quality customer service

TQM

Total quality management (TQM) is a system devised by W. Edwards Deming for improving quality control at the level of production. In order for it to work, employees need to be given specific and comprehensive rules for self-evaluation. It should not be the job of supervisors to enforce quality control measures. Instead, management is charged with creating and implementing the overall organizational mission.

A TQM program typically begins by creating worker participation programs and policies, giving employees the opportunity to provide feedback and ask questions. Employees should be given autonomy and invited to discuss quality issues when necessary. When the total quality management system is successful, one result is improved morale among employees.

Cite Deming's 14-Point TQM

"Create constancy of purpose for improvement of products and service." Ensure that the focus of the business is on creating and maintaining jobs:

- "*Adopt the new philosophy*." Provide excellent service and a quality product
- "*Cease dependence on mass inspection*." Improve the process and reduce the need for inspection
- "*End the practice of awarding business on price tag alone*." It is better to have quality materials and maintain steady relationships along the supply chain
- "Improve constantly the system of production and service"
- "Institute training"
- "Institute leadership"
- "*Drive out fear*." Empower subordinates to ask questions
- "Break down barriers between staff areas." Promote cooperation
- "Eliminate slogans, exhortations, and targets for the workforce"
- "*Eliminate numerical quotas*." Rigid quotas lead to corner-cutting and inefficiencies
- "*Remove barriers to pride of workmanship*." Give employees what they need to perform well
- "Institute a vigorous program of education and retraining"
- "*Take action to accomplish the transformation*." A sufficient number of managers and workers must be on board

Technology

Technology is the use of science and technical skill to create new processes, products, or services.

Process Innovations

Process innovations are new or improved ways of making and distributing products.

Product Innovations

Product innovations are new or improved products or services.

Technology Life Cycle

Technology life cycle are the trend of innovation, in which it begins as a new idea, eventually saturates the market, and ends up being replaced by something new.

CIO

Chief information officer (CIO) is the manager in charge of coordinating information technology.

Technical Innovator

Technical innovator is a person who comes up with a new technology or is capable of using it.

Product Champion

Product champion is a person who encourages other members of an organization to use some new technology.

Development Project

Development project is an intentional effort to develop and implement new processes.

Sociotechnical Systems

Sociotechnical systems are combinations of social and technical efficiencies that are used to improve systems.

Stages of Technological Products

There are four categories for technologies:

- *Base technologies*: used industry-wide
- *Key technologies*: used by some in an industry; users obtain some competitive advantage
- *Pacing technologies*: competitive advantage is not yet obvious, but potential is apparent
- *Emerging technologies*: not yet proven to benefit the user, though managers are keeping close watch

Manager Assessment

Most managers begin their assessment with a technology audit, which identifies the equipment essential to the success of the firm. Before making any subsequent investments in technology, a manager should consider the following:

- Basic operational needs
- Economic viability
- Organizational suitability and ability to develop technological competency
- Technological feasibility
- Anticipated market receptiveness

Benchmarking is a good way to identify technology needs. Another system, called scanning, focuses on emerging technologies, and is used to keep organizations current.

ACQUIRING NEW TECHNOLOGIES

Internal development is perhaps the best way, provided that the business has sufficient resources to afford research and development. Internally developed technologies are easier to keep under the control of the organization.

Contracted development is when other businesses are paid to develop and test new technologies.

Acquisition of the owner of proprietary technology is the purchase of a tech company or merely the purchase of shares in a tech company.

Purchase technologies that have already been developed may be available on the open market. Of course, there is unlikely to be any great competitive advantage in obtaining widely-available technologies.

Licensing some technologies are not available for purchase, but can be licensed for a small fee.

Technology trading is when companies may be able to learn how to make new technologies by observing their use in other firms.

Research partnerships and joint ventures are agreements with other organizations to develop new technologies. Joint ventures tend to be more enduring than research partnerships.

APPROACHES TO ORGANIZE FOR INNOVATION

Most companies find that continuous innovation is the best way to stay competitive over the long term. The constant refinement of existing processes and services is known as "intrapreneurship". It is good to establish an organizational climate in which employees feel comfortable sharing ideas and brainstorming.

One creative company, 3M, has outlined six basic rules for creating a climate of innovation: setting creativity goals, committing time and money to research and development, encouraging intrapreneurship, facilitating rather than obstructing, staying focused on the customer, and tolerating failure. Only flexible and organic organizations are able to maintain continuous innovation; bureaucracies are more likely to remain stagnant. Some companies establish special "greenhouse" divisions for the particular purpose of research and innovation. The nation of Japan has even legislated that scientists be allowed to spend 20% of their time on secret research, a policy known as angura. A pro-innovation culture tends to boost general morale and increase skills across the board.

ORGANIZATIONAL CHANGE

The business world is always shifting. In order to stay on top of the global market, managers have to adapt constantly. The goal for many businesses is to become world-class. World-class organizations have characteristics in common. They have "stretch" goals that are challenging yet attainable. They are constantly innovating and developing solutions to internal as well as external problems. Nevertheless, they maintain a central vision. A company becomes world class by focusing its efforts on customers and offering employees a challenging and rewarding workplace. These organizations usually have flexible structures and an easy flow of information.

ORGANIZATIONAL DEVELOPMENT

Behavioral science can be used to improve business structures, a process known as organizational development. The intention of these efforts is to maximize the potential of employees. A full-scale organizational change will probably entail alterations in every department of the business, as well as maintenance of these changes in every different unit. The changes should be specially selected to be in agreement with the overall organizational mission. The implementation of changes can be improved by:

- Creating desire for reform within the organization
- Outlining a clear vision
- Establishing a respected team to manage change
- Ensuring that progress is tangible to all employees
- Maintaining constant communication with employees
- Consolidating the gains made because of implemented changes

Hawthorne Studies and the Hawthorne Effect

Between 1924 and 1936, the Western Electric Company performed a series of workplace experiments outside of Chicago. These inquiries into the correlation between working conditions and productivity were known as the Hawthorne Studies. At first, these studies were led by Harvard researchers, including Elton Mayo and Fritz Roethlisberger. The opening set of experiments had to do with lighting: the researchers raised and lowered the lights as they measured the productivity of a group of sample workers. The disappointing result of this first experiment was that the variations in productivity were most likely related to the observation of the scientists than to the lighting. This observer effect is known now as the Hawthorne Effect. Indeed, the primary result of the Hawthorne Studies was the idea that social factors contribute more than environmental factors to productivity.

Terms

Competitive Advantage

Competitive advantage is the capacity of a business to create a product with a lower cost, better features, better quality, or better customer care

Competitive Scope

Competitive scope is the section in a market targeted by a company, in terms of product development and distribution.

Cost Focus

Cost focus is the strategy of augmenting competitive advantage by diminishing the area of distribution, which in turn cuts costs.

Cost Leadership

Cost leadership is a strategy of improving sales by maintaining a lower cost.

Differentiation

Differentiation is the process of distinguishing a product or service from its competition.

Focused Differentiation

Focused differentiation is a combination of unique products or services and limited geographical distribution.

Bureaucracy

Bureaucracy is an organizational structure featuring specialization, rigid hierarchy, explicit rules, and codified methods of selecting personnel.

Open System

Open system is a system of organization in which external forces can have an impact.

Synergistic Effect

Synergistic effect is the combined impacts of the functions of each specialized part of an organization.

Span of Control

Span of control is the number of employees who report directly to a specific manager.

Technology

Technology is a set of equipment and procedures for converting raw materials into finished products.

Technological Imperative

Technological imperative is the perceived correlation between complexity in technology and organizational structure.

Adaptive Learning

Adaptive learning is one of the first stages in organizational development, in which adjustments for the business climate prove successful.

Generative Learning

Generative learning is a stage of organizational evolution in which managers learn the true effects of implemented business systems.

Gantt Chart

Gantt chart is named for its inventor, Henri Gantt, one of the early leaders of the scientific management movement, is a chart that lists and schedules necessary tasks, including expected completion times for each task and for the product as a whole.

Production Management

Production management is the science of management related to production technology and the path from innovation to production.

Operations Management

Operations management is the signs of management related to non-manufacturing tasks, as for instance employee training, purchasing, inventory and financial operations.

Information System

Information system is a digital system of record keeping, which allows management to make informed decisions and helps employees at all levels to access important data.

General Environment

General environment is the comprehensive climate in which decision-making takes place.

Task Environment

Task environment is the set of environmental factors that directly relate to organizational success.

Core Competencies

Core competencies are the skills and knowledge unique to a particular business, which gives it a competitive advantage.

Competitive Advantage

Competitive advantage is the unique ability or position held by a company because of its core competencies.

Industry Environment

Industry environment is the competition, customer base, product lines, and other characteristics in which a business operates.

Strategic Intent

Strategic intent is the intentions of both the stakeholders and employees of the business over the long term.

Strategic Thinking

Strategic thinking is the capacity of management to accurately assess competition and craft appropriate strategies that take advantage of core competencies.

Business Model

Business model is the set of processes used to make an organization viable; should respect the content of explicit goals.

Line Departments

Line departments are responsible for the most important tasks completed by the company.

Staff Departments

Staff departments are trained to provide assistance to line departments.

Functional Organizations

Functional organizations are departments are organized by function and necessary skills.

Divisional Organizations

Divisional organizations feature several different product line divisions, each of which contains the entire line of production, from purchasing to sales. Some divisional organizations have specific units to serve individual markets.

Matrix Organizations

Matrix organizations combine functional and divisional structures. In such an organization, some employees may be responsible to multiple managers, and employees from different departments may be grouped to complete a project.

Network Organizations

Network organizations assemblages of single-function businesses brought together to accomplish a specific goal; one business is typically in charge of managing the relationships.

Scale Economies

Scale economies are a creation of profit by producing at high volume and low cost. In most cases, only very large firms can create scale economies.

Diseconomies of Scale

Diseconomies of scale are the costs that are unique to large companies, as for instance administrative confusion, reduced speed of communication, and missed opportunities due to lack of agility.

Economies of Scope

Economies of scope are savings created by using materials and equipment for multiple processes.

Downsizing

Downsizing is termination of employees, elimination of jobs, and compression of hierarchies within an organization, especially when it is done to improve efficiency.

Rightsizing

Rightsizing: adjustments to the size of an organization that place it in an optimal position to succeed; could include enlarging or diminishing the size of the organization.

Survivor's Syndrome

Survivor's syndrome is a phenomenon that occurs after layoffs and terminations, in which the remaining employees are paranoid, risk-averse, and depressed.

Chain of Command

Chain of command is the paths of authority in an organization, consisting of a series of superior-subordinate relationships.

Line Position

Line position is any position within the chain of command that directly contributes to the completion of the organizational goals.

Staff Position

Staff position is any position that leads, assists, or supports the line positions.

Departmentalization

Departmentalization is the process of placing jobs in categories according to their customer base, geographical location, or function.

Functional Departmentalization

Functional departmentalization is the process of placing jobs in categories according to their function, such as marketing, manufacturing, and sales.

Product Departmentalization

Product departmentalization is the process of sorting jobs according to their product line.

Customer Departmentalization

Customer departmentalization is the process of sorting jobs according to the customers they serve, for instance, some manufacturers have different departments for dealing with corporate and private customers.

Geographic Departmentalization

Geographic departmentalization is the sorting of jobs according to the geographical region served; this process is especially useful for very large international corporations.

EEO

Equal employment opportunity (EEO) is a foundation of business ethics in the United States, whereby all people are guaranteed an equal chance for employment, regardless of race, religion, gender, etc.

Affirmative Action

Affirmative action is a strategy for increasing the presence of minorities and underrepresented groups in business, by giving special preference to them in hiring.

Human Resource Planning

Human resource planning is a process of predicting and planning for employee needs.

Human Resource Management

Human resource management is the set of processes devoted to the hiring, training, and retention of employees, including preparation of compensation packages, performance evaluations, employee discipline, collective bargaining, arbitration, and terminations.

Organizational Environment

Job Satisfaction, QWL, and Psychological Contracts

When employees are more satisfied, they do a better job, and the company makes more money. Happy employees are less likely to be absent or quit and tend to cost the business less in insurance. For this reason, many companies create quality of work life (QWL) programs. These programs ensure that employees are receiving fair compensation, a safe workplace, opportunities for personal growth, the chance to be themselves, respect for their personal lives, privacy, and faith in management.

Companies also now think not only about formal contracts, but about psychological contracts with employees; psychological contracts are the role expectations held by employees and employers. For instance, employees expect to be treated fairly and given chances to succeed, and employers expect honest effort and hard work.

Effects of Laws and Regulations

Business is both constrained and liberated by the laws and regulations of the United States. The laws protect property rights, but forbid what they define as unfair business practices.

International businesses generally feel that the safety and security of working in the United States vastly outweigh the restrictions. The United States does, however, maintain a number of federal organizations for the purpose of investigating business. Among these are the Equal Employment Opportunity Commission, Environmental Protection Agency, Occupational Health and Safety Administration, and Securities and Exchange Commission. These departments of the federal government investigate and prosecute business crimes. Of course, in the long run businesses benefit from the creation of a fair economic climate. The United States manages entrants to the American market in such a way as to benefit domestic business, and often provides direct subsidies to American companies.

General Economic Environment Impact

The general economic environment for business consists of both the economy within the United States and the economy abroad. It has a huge impact on business decisions. Interest rates determine purchases, availability of capital, demand, and prices.

Unemployment affects wages, availability of employees, and demand for products and services. The costs of energy and medical treatment affect the cost of running a company. Also, changes in the value of a dollar have obvious effects on business. Moreover, some businesses are closely tied to the markets for housing, precious metals, stocks, and bonds. The acceleration of the securities trading markets has made it increasingly tempting for managers to engage in morally dubious behavior in the interest of short-term profits.

Organization Culture

The culture of an organization is the set of assumptions, goals, and values shared by all of the members. If the organization culture is strong and positive, it can have a profound and wonderful impact on employees. If the culture is strong and negative, on the other hand, it can discourage employees. Also, if the culture of an organization remains stagnant for a long time, it can have a deleterious effect on employees.

When companies merge or one company acquires another, there is an inevitable clash between cultures. It is the job of the remaining management to harmonize whatever differences may exist between the respective organizations. If organizational culture is weak, employees will be confused and will have differing priorities. As much as possible, the behaviors prescribed by the company's policies should align with organizational culture.

Organization Cultures

The following factors contribute to the formation of organizational culture:

- Corporate mission statements and organizational goals, and in particular, the degree to which employees recognize and endorse them
- Business practices: the decisions, strategies, and customer service policies of the company
- Symbols, rites, and ceremonies, in particular, the sorts of deeds and accomplishments that are rewarded or punished
- Myths, legends, and true stories about the firm's past

An organizational culture can be defined by the presence of flexibility or control, as well as an internal or external focus:

- *Group culture (flexible, internal):* leaders are like heads of a family, striving to maximize the potential of each subordinate
- *Hierarchical culture (inflexible, internal):* based on strict rules and guidelines; leaders reinforce these rules
- *Adhocracy (flexible, external):* leaders encourage innovation and set up structures to enable creativity
- *Rational culture (inflexible, external):* leaders focus on profit and market share, and employees are encouraged to be competitive and goal-oriented

Management of Corporate Culture Change

Perhaps the best way for an organization to evolve is to consciously change its culture. For instance, in recent years many companies have adopted a customer-focused culture, when in the past they may have focused on productivity or efficiency. It may be necessary to teach the new values explicitly, rather than just changing the policies in writing. Management may elect to outline the new culture in a face-to-face meeting, or it may prefer to reinforce the new behavior with rewards. Sometimes, an organization hires new employees, trains them in the new culture, and then encourages them to spread what they have learned to the other employees. In any case, it often takes a long time for organizational culture to change in any discernible way.

Workforce Reduction

When an employee lacks skills or does not perform well, it may be necessary to terminate him or her. When companies merge or are divested, they often have to lay off employees. A responsible employer will grant severance pay and give the terminated employee some help in finding another job. Although a 1908 Supreme Court ruling declared that employment can be terminated "for good cause, for no cause, or even for cause morally wrong," many states have modified this idea.

For instance, employees who are terminated because they served jury duty, blew the whistle, or refused to break the law may find remedy in many states. Also, many unions have contracts limiting the circumstances under which members can be terminated. When arbitration is necessary, the company will fare better if it can demonstrate a good faith effort to help the employee before termination.

UNITED STATES LAWS AFFECT EMPLOYMENT OPPORTUNITY

Fair Labor Standards Act (1938): divided employees into exempt, such as managers and others who could not receive overtime pay, and non-exempt, who could.

Equal Pay Act (1963): outlawed pay discrimination based on gender.

Civil Rights Act (1964): outlawed employment discrimination based on race, sex, ethnicity, nationality, or religion; Title VII outlawed discrimination in recruiting, hiring, termination, promotion, compensation, and training.

Age Discrimination in Employment Act (1967): outlawed employment discrimination against those over 40 and limited mandatory retirement.

Vocational Rehabilitation Act (1973): enforced affirmative action for federal employers and contractors with respect to disability.

Americans with Disabilities Act (1990): outlawed employment discrimination against the disabled; definition of disability expanded to include cancer patients in remission, those afflicted with AIDS, alcoholics, and drug abusers.

Civil Rights Act (1991): strengthened anti-discriminatory legislation and redefined punishments for violators.

Family and Medical Leave Act (1991): asserted that employees with medical or family needs should receive twelve weeks unpaid leave without threat of termination.

COMPENSATION AND BENEFITS LEGAL ISSUES

Fair Labor Standards Act (FLSA), 1938: categorized exempt and non-exempt employees and established minimum wage, child labor, and maximum hour laws.

Equal Pay Act (EPA), 1963: outlawed pay discrimination based on gender, but allowed it in relation to merit, incentive systems, market demand, seniority, etc.

Comparable-worth doctrine: a woman who does work of equal worth to that of a man deserves to be paid as well as the man. There are no statutes requiring comparable-worth compensation, but some laws support this doctrine.

Employee Retirement Income Security Act (ERISA), 1974: employees who have earned the right to draw retirement benefits must be given them; bankrupt and defaulting companies will have their employee pensions paid by the government.

Pregnancy Discrimination Act (1978): categorized pregnancy as a disability and entitled pregnant women to the benefits afforded other disabled people.

HEALTH AND SAFETY LAWS AND CONCERNS

The Occupational Safety and Health Act (OSHA) assert rules for workplace safety, as for instance mandatory onsite inspections and record-keeping related to deaths and injuries. Many professions remain dangerous. Coal miners, for instance, still die every year, although the numbers are greatly diminished from the hundreds of casualties suffered during the 1960s.

To maintain workplace safety, it is essential for employees to speak up. There is legislation to protect workers who blow the whistle on unsafe working conditions. For instance, it is not legal for these employees to be fired for alerting authorities to conditions that could result in injury or death.

US Labor Laws

National Labor Relations Act, otherwise known as the Wagner Act (1935): legalized labor unions, outlawed several employer practices related to labor, and created the National Labor Relations Board. This act basically unionized the country overnight and enabled collective bargaining to begin winning victories for workers, such as minimum wage and maternity leave.

Labor-Management Relations Act

Labor-Management Relations Act, otherwise known as the Taft-Hartley Act (1947)_protected management by outlawing some labor union practices, allowing workers to decertify their union, and reinforcing free speech rights.

Labor-Management Reporting and Disclosure Act, otherwise known as the Landrum-Griffin Act (1959): created a bill of rights for union members, including union reporting requirements and control over union dues.

Workers Join Unions

Unions increase the average level of pay for their members and negotiate with management from a position of power. Unions are able to make bad working conditions better and protect the rights of workers. In most cases, a union gets its foot in the door by sending a representative to teach workers the advantages of union membership. Workers are given authorization cards, which they can use to indicate whether they would like to be certified as union members.

When at least 30% of the employees in a shop sign the cards, an election is administered by the National Labor Relations Board. Management must either recognize the union without requiring the election, consent to the election, or dispute the number of signed cards. A certification election is performed with a secret ballot, with the winner only needing a simple majority. If the union wins, management and the union must obtain a collective bargaining agreement or contract, and the union is therefore certified as the bargaining unit representative.

Union Shops and Collective Bargaining

In union shops, employees are required to join the union after a certain interval.

Collective bargaining usually occurs every three years and entails the negotiation of wages, benefits, hours, and working conditions.

Economic Strikes, Arbitration, Wildcat Strikes, and Right-to-Work States

It is legal for workers to go on economic strikes to force management to agree to their terms. However, striking has become an unpopular option, because management has demonstrated the ability to hire replacement workers and wait out the strikers. A strike that is against the rules of the union contract is known as a wildcat strike. Contract disputes between management and unions often end up in arbitration, in which a neutral third party agreed upon by both sides settles the conflict. Right-to-work states, which are mostly in the South, forbid union shops and keep employees who do not join a union from being discriminated against.

Future of Unionization

It seems that labor union membership in the United States peaked a little after World War II, when it was at about 33%. Now, union membership is about 12%. One reason for this is that there are simply fewer blue-collar jobs and fewer permanent relationships between employers and employees. Over time, unions have had to adjust their policies to include women, government employees, and older workers. There remains a role for unions in advocating for workers and improving conditions in the workplace. The relationship of unions is likely to become less adversarial with management in the future, as more and more companies have come to the realization that satisfied employees are good for business.

Political-Legal Environment

Although many corporations claim to be restrained by government regulations, it is the government that creates a fair and safe business climate in which corporations can operate. Also, the government has been responsible for many direct subsidies to struggling industries, as for instance the airlines. Government infrastructure programs make it possible for companies to ship goods all over the country. After the recent financial crisis, the government is looking to expand its regulation of securities markets. It is likely that government regulation will increase in response to new and more complex corporate structures and practices.

Diverse Workforce Management

The labor force of the United States is very diverse, and companies must learn to harness the power of this diversity if they are to survive and thrive. Moreover, companies that fail to honor diversity could be found to violate American law. It is especially important for managers to be sensitive to cultural differences. Companies must have procedures for hiring, training, advancing, and challenging employees from all different backgrounds, and must ensure that their policies do not disrespect cultures. Globalization has encouraged many companies to improve their diversity training programs, and in the process, many companies have discovered new and better ways to access foreign markets.

Diversity in the United States Today

There are almost unlimited ways in which the American labor force is diverse: race, gender, nationality, education, age, socioeconomic group, sexual orientation, religion, and military experience, just to name a few. In a real sense, all employees are diverse, and so a manager must develop the ability to relate to individuals at their own level. Although white persons currently make up about 80% of the American workforce, this proportion is expected to drop in the coming decades. In particular, there are expected to be larger percentages of women, African-American, and Hispanic employees. At the present time, 15% of the American labor force was born in another country. Throughout the history of the United States, immigrants have proven to be among the most innovative entrepreneurs, and this trend is expected to continue.

Disabled Acceptance in the US Workforce

In the United States, the largest unemployed minority is the disabled. Eighteen percent of American citizens are disabled in some way, and 6% have disabilities that are so severe they have a hard time getting a job. Nevertheless, half of disabled Americans are employed.

The Americans with Disabilities Act prohibited discrimination against the disabled and issued specific mandates for disability-friendly construction. Nevertheless, the awesome potential of many disabled people has yet to be tapped. In particular, employers who hire the disabled find that they experience less turnover and greater employee reliability. Also, some businesses receive tax credits for hiring the disabled.

Employer Strategies to Recruit Workers

The American workforce is getting older: 40% of workers are 45 years or older and 70% of this plan on working after they retire. Although some businesses shy away from hiring older employees, these workers tend to have more knowledge, be more dependable, and leave their jobs less often than younger workers. Some businesses have started offering phased retirement programs, so that older employees can gradually reduce their hours while still providing the business with their expertise.

Many younger workers, meanwhile, are considered high maintenance because they have been raised to expect work experiences that are challenging and inspiring. Many employers become frustrated managing the outsized expectations of these young employees. Nevertheless, companies need to hire new employees, and many now use social networking tools like Facebook to recruit prospective employees.

Equal Employment Opportunity and Affirmative Action Programs

Affirmative action began as a mandate of the employment laws enforced by the Equal Employment Opportunity Commission. The goal of affirmative action was to give long-excluded groups a boost into employment. Despite generally positive effects from affirmative action, however, employment discrimination is still a problem in the United States. Many businesses have yet to realize that diversity is not just a mandate, but a recipe for economic success. To harness the power of diversity, a business needs to develop programs that take advantage of differences in talent and perspective. One hallmark of such diversity-positive programs is an emphasis on communication.

Diverse Workforce Competitive Advantages

Numerous studies have shown that more diverse companies tend to perform better over the long term. Diverse employers seem better able to recruit, retain, and inspire their employees. Employees are more likely to give their all for an organization which they feel respects their background. Companies with a diverse labor force also seem to have a better understanding of the diverse marketplace.

In particular, the presence of women and minorities in the sales and marketing departments seems to be tied to greater rates of sale to those demographics. Diverse companies demonstrate greater levels of innovation and are less likely to succumb to groupthink. Also, diverse organizations seem to be more attuned to changes in the marketplace and are more likely to have a flexible organizational structure.

Diversity Workforce Challenges

False or Unconsidered Assumptions

A manager's unconscious prejudices can lead to poor decisions, especially in hiring; for instance, a manager may assume that a woman or a small man is incapable of performing a job requiring physical strength.

Diminished Cohesiveness

Diminished cohesiveness because employees come from different backgrounds, they have less in common and find it harder to get along; in this situation, it is essential to get the entire group united behind the organizational mission.

Communication Difficulties

Manager's waste time repeating themselves and elaborating on simple instructions.

Lack of social comfort and trust: employees find it difficult to relate to one another and feel ill at ease in one another's presence.

Stereotyping

Stereotyping employees assume that the members of another cultural or social group share similar characteristics.

Monolithic Organizations

There is very little cultural integration in a monolithic organization, because there is very little cultural differentiation between employees. In a monolithic organization, the only minority employees tend to be in very low-status jobs. In the United States, however, most companies went from being monolithic to being pluralistic during the 1960s and 1970s.

Pluralistic Organizations

A pluralistic organization eliminates discrimination and employs people from all races, ethnicities, and genders. Even within a pluralistic organization, though, it is not unusual for similar employees to be in the same fields or to cluster socially.

Multicultural Organizations

In a multicultural organization, diversity is an avowed goal and minorities are present at all levels. Indeed, managers make a point of using the diverse backgrounds of employees to the advantage of the firm. Such organizations eliminate prejudice and discrimination, and are better at helping employees reach their full potential.

Diversity Approaches

Homogeneity

Homogeneity (melting pot myth, all people are the same.

Similarity

Similarity (similarity myth), everybody is just like me.

Parochialism

Parochialism (only-one-way myth), the way of this community is the only way we know about.

Ethnocentrism

Ethnocentrism (one-way-best myth), the way of this community is the best possible way.

Heterogeneity

Heterogeneity (cultural pluralism), there are a lot of cross-cultural differences between groups.

Similarity and Difference

Similarity and difference is the acknowledgement of the inevitability of similarities and differences between cultures.

Equifinality

Equifinality when there are a number of different ways for various cultures to arrive at the same ends.

Culture Contingency

Culture contingency is when there are plenty of different ways to achieve goals, and the right choice depends on the culture of the relevant people.

Multicultural Organization Development

Obtaining the commitment of top management is perhaps best accomplished by tying compensation to diversity. Managers should be role models for multiculturalism and should be encouraged to divert sufficient funds to maintain a diverse workforce.

Organizational assessment, in particular, workforce interaction analysis can be used to improve human resource policy and employee behavior with respect to multicultural issues.

Attracting employees, recruiting techniques should be sufficient to hire minority employees; whenever possible, employees should be given the option to telecommute or use a compressed workweek and flexible schedule; employees should be given parental leave and access to child care.

Training employees, emphasis on interpersonal skills, such as active listening and feedback; employees should be taught to identify and question their own assumptions.

Retaining employees, management should be responsible for maintaining diversity.

Mentoring programs are a good way for women and minority employees to stay involved.

Other ways include an emphasis on career development, socialization into organizational culture, and instruction on company politics.

Global Economy, Global Boom, and Global Opportunities

A number of factors, such as immigration, technology, and joint ventures, have given birth to a global economy. Almost every country in the world participates in international business. There are thousands of multinational corporations whose supply chains extend beyond the borders of their home country. This global boom has increased customer expectations and raised the level of competition worldwide. Increasingly, businesses are required to deliver a world-class product or service. These challenges are accompanied by great opportunities, however: businesses have been able to reduce costs and outsource production to countries in which wages are lower. These outsourcing arrangements can be beneficial for both countries involved.

MNCs and Global Corporations

Multinational companies (MNCs) are based in one country, but have some operations or departments in other countries. For instance, a multinational company might be based in the United States but have its manufacturing hubs in India. A global corporation is slightly different. Global corporations are more scattered and tend to have the entire world as their market. Whereas a multinational company might base some operations in another country but do most of its business in the domestic market, a global corporation is more flexible and is able to shift its operations around the world to take advantage of economic trends. A global corporation is likely to have one strategy for doing business, whereas a multinational company may have different strategies for each country in which it operates.

International Business

Exporting

Exporting is the sale of domestic goods in a foreign country. This is the easiest way to participate in international business, and there are firms that specialize in marketing other companies' products abroad.

Licensing

Licensing is a licensor company gives a licensee company permission to sell its products under the licensor's name, in exchange for a percentage of sales. Sometimes, such a trade agreement is little more than an excuse for the licensee to obtain trade secrets and then sell the product itself after the contract expires.

Trading Companies

Trading companies are businesses that serve as intermediaries by purchasing goods and shipping them for sale abroad. In exchange for taking on the risk of the manufacturer, the trading company gets part of the profits. These businesses become expert on quality, price expectations, foreign exchange, distribution, and markets.

Countertrading Approach

Countertrading is a bartering system that enables cash-poor countries to participate in the global market. Countries that have poor exports require export-heavy countries to purchase their goods before they will allow goods from the other countries to be sold there. This strategy has been used by many of the former Soviet states, which do not have enough money to purchase Western goods because they do not export enough of their own merchandise. These agreements can be successful, although it is sometimes difficult to assess the value of merchandise, and in some cases, the United States has been left with worthless goods that cannot be sold. When it works, however, countertrading is a good tool for bringing developing economies into the global market.

Joint Ventures and Strategic Alliances

Joint ventures are partnerships between companies in two different countries. These can be very useful when one company is unfamiliar with a foreign market and wants to take advantage of the expertise of a company based there. Also, some governments limit the foreign ownership of businesses, so a business based abroad may have no option for operating there other than a joint venture. Many companies use joint ventures to gain access to suppliers, distributors, and technology.

A strategic alliance, on the other hand, is a more involved partnership. Strategic alliances are long-term agreements between companies in different countries. There is a great degree of risk involved in a strategic alliance, so it must be investigated thoroughly.

Direct Ownership Approach

Many businesses operate in foreign countries by simply buying companies and facilities there. This can be very expensive, but massive American multinational companies like Ford and 3M use it to great success. Indeed, the American brands of Magnavox and Pillsbury are actually subsidiaries of foreign multinational corporations.

When a company directly owns foreign businesses, it does not have to pay export costs or tariffs. Also, manufacturing costs tend to be lower. By paying taxes in the foreign country, the owning company develops a good relationship with the host government. Of course, the direct ownership approach can run into trouble when the foreign government or economy is unstable. Also, these arrangements can be difficult to exit when problems arise.

Understanding Cultural Difference

In order for international management to work, managers need to understand differences in culture. For instance, even simple things like personal space and body language are treated quite differently abroad, and a manager who is ignorant of these simple customs may run afoul of trading partners. More technically, the customs of business are likely to be different abroad.

In some countries, price-fixing and bribery are the norms, and it may be necessary to work through a middleman. Before entering a foreign market, American businesses must do significant research on local customs and economic trends. Also, employees who will be handling international business must be screened and trained. Employees who will be working in non-English speaking countries should be fluent in the relevant foreign language.

Economic and Technological Environments

Before a company can successfully operate in a foreign country, it needs to have a firm grasp of the level of technological development and general economic environment there. If the economy in the foreign country is not stable, or if the population is not large enough to provide a sufficient market, the investment may be pointless. One indicator of income in a foreign market is gross domestic product (GDP), which is the market value of all goods and services produced in the country in a year. If the ratio of GDP to population is very low, then the standard of living enjoyed by the citizens there may not be high enough to warrant market entry. Also, levels of education and infrastructure developments suggest the health of a foreign market.

Political and Legal Environments

Before entering a foreign market, an American business will survey the legal and political climate for business there. For instance, some countries establish quotas on the amount of goods that can be imported or exported, which would put obvious restrictions on the viability of doing business there. Countries also may place taxes or embargoes on certain goods. Some countries have draconian customs policies, which can drastically slow down the transport of goods. If the political situation in a foreign country is unstable, businesses cannot be assured that their interests will be protected. In the past, political chaos has led to the seizure of foreign-owned assets and the destruction of private property. A stable political landscape reassures foreign investors.

US Laws Affect How US Companies Engage in International Business

Web-Pomerene Export Trade Act (1918): allows US businesses to violate antitrust laws in the development of certain export markets so long as the businesses do not compete unfairly or reduce competition in the domestic market.

Foreign Corrupt Practices Act (1977): forbids US businesses from offering bribes to foreign officials. Offending companies could be subjected to $1 million in penalties, and offending individuals could be subject to five years in prison and up to $10,000 in fines.

Export Trading Companies Act (1982): promoted the formation of export trading companies by allowing banks to form joint ventures and eliminating antitrust barriers.

Despite the above legislation, some American businesses continue to exploit lax foreign regulation and sell dangerous products abroad. In particular, developing and Third World nations are too often the market for harmful chemicals and electronic trash.

INTERNATIONAL TRADE ORGANIZATIONS TIMELINE

1944: International Monetary Fund established to ease trade among nations and provide loans to countries looking to join the international market.

1946: World Bank created as a lender to developing nations.

1947: General Agreement on Tariffs and Trade (GATT) created to reduce the barriers to trade, in particular tariffs.

1964: after the Trade Expansion Act of 1962, the Kennedy Round agrees to a 40% decrease in tariffs.

1973: the Tokyo Round initiates a six-year period in which tariffs are reduced by 30%; this period also saw a virtual elimination of import quotas and customs bureaucracy.

1989: over one hundred nations pledge in the Uruguay Round to eliminate farm subsidies and arbitrate international disputes according to a standard system.

1995: GATT is replaced by the World Trade Organization, which at present has 128 member nations.

July 2004: the Doha Round improves market access for developing nations, with the intention of improving trade.

NAFTA

The North American Free Trade Agreement (NAFTA) was created in 1992, when Mexico, Canada, and the United States agreed to eliminate almost all tariffs and non-tariff trade barriers between them. This trilateral agreement was spurred by complementary needs:

- Mexico had resources and people but no outlet to use them
- Canada had natural resources but few people to harvest them
- United States had businesses that needed natural resources and cheap manufacturing venues

The agreement has mostly been a success: jobs have been created and inflation has diminished. Between 1993 and 2005, all countries experienced GDP growth, more than 20 million jobs were created, and trade among the three nations rose by 173%. One loser has been the Mexican farmer, as the swamping of the Mexican market by United States agribusiness has been overwhelming. In the United States, the loss of manufacturing jobs is often blamed on NAFTA.

EU

The European Union (EU), formerly the European Community (EC), was created as part of the Maastricht Treaty in 1993. In 2010, the group comprised 27 nations. The first to join were mostly western European nations, but now the group includes such disparate countries as Cyprus, Latvia, and Ireland. The EU combines supranationalism with intergovernmentalism. One of the purposes of the union is to allow the easy passage of people and materials. Also, sixteen nations currently use the euro as their currency.

Taken together, the nominal GDP of the EU nations is the largest economy in the world. Indeed, the EU is the biggest trading partner for growing exporters such as China and India.

APEC

The Asian Pacific Economic Cooperation (APEC) allows 27 nations to trade and develop their internal markets. The members of this group include Russia, Japan, China, Hong Kong, Taiwan, South Korea, Vietnam, Malaysia, Singapore, the Philippines, Australia, New Zealand, Thailand, Canada, the United States, Mexico, Peru, and Chile. The group is even considering allowing some countries that do not border on the Pacific Ocean, such as India and Pakistan, to join the group. Every year, the members of APEC gather and negotiate trade agreements. They also discuss issues, such as terrorism and political instability that could potentially disrupt trade. As Japanese firms such as Canon and Sony have grown, the importance of APEC for the United States has grown as well.

CAFTA and Western Hemisphere Free Trade Groups

The United States joined the meetings of the Central America Free Trade Agreement in 2005. CAFTA, which includes Costa Rica, El Salvador, Honduras, Nicaragua, and Guatemala, was originally formed to protect the rights of workers, although critics charged that the organization was largely unsuccessful in this respect.

The Dominican Republic has subsequently joined the group, which is now often known as DR-CAFTA. Some pairs of nations, such as the United States and Panama, have elected to create bilateral agreements rather than work through CAFTA.

The Caribbean Community, or CARICOM, is a trade organization uniting nations such as Belize and Haiti. Mercosur is a bloc of South American nations, although it may be rendered obsolete soon by the creation of a Free Trade Area of the Americas that includes both North and South America.

Ethnocentrism and Culture Shock

Despite the fact that 15% of employee transfers are to overseas locations, between 20% and 70% of these transfers fail. Culture shock and marital problems are the most common reasons for the failure of overseas transfers. People have an unhelpful tendency towards ethnocentrism, which is the idea that one's own culture is superior to others or is the standard for all others. Employees who are excessively ethnocentric will likely feel alienated or disoriented in foreign surroundings. Geert Hofstede outlined four dimensions of cultural difference:

- Power distance: the degree to which a culture accepts power inequalities in corporate life
- Individualism-collectivism: the degree to which the members of a culture can act autonomously rather than as a group
- Uncertainty avoidance: the degree to which the members of a culture are made uncomfortable by uncertainty
- Masculinity-femininity: the degree to which a culture places so-called masculine values (money, status) over female qualities (beauty, kindness)

Ethical Issues in International Management

Ethics can vary from country to country, so businesses must take care not to run afoul of local customs or values. There are many nations, for instance, in which bribery is very common, and despite the Foreign Corrupt Practices Act of 1977, there are still many American executives who look the other way when their subordinates bribe foreign officials. Indeed, one poll found that 20% of American managers believed it was always acceptable to offer bribes to foreign officials. It is allowed to give small gifts to lower-level officials, so long as the value of the gift is below a certain dollar amount and the gift does not influence negotiations. In 2002, the Sarbanes-Oxley Act strengthened bribery law enforcement, in part by forcing companies to establish and maintain ethics programs. This act and others rest on the principle that across cultures, people honor respect, fairness, honesty, compassion, and responsibility.

OPEC, EFTA, and LAFTA

OPEC, EFTA, and LAFTA trade organizations, all established in 1960.

OPEC

Organization of Petroleum Exporting Countries (OPEC): a cartel of twelve Middle Eastern, African, and South American countries that produce oil. OPEC's intention is to regulate the supplies and prices of oil and to guarantee profits for the members and steady supply to customers.

EFTA

European Free Trade Association (EFTA): connected to the European Union, this organization was devised as an alternative to the European Economic Community (EEC). Unlike the EEC, the EFTA did not have a common external customs tariff. The EFTA originally had seven member nations, but now has only four.

LAFTA

Latin American Free Trade Association (LAFTA): a free trade association formed by eleven nations in Latin America, the group has been able to increase investment, reduce costs, and improve productive capacity. Since 1980, this organization has been known as the Association Latinoamericana de Integracion (ALADI).

Terms

Acquisition

Acquisition is a purchase of one company by another.

Buffering

Buffering is storage of extra resources for possible times of need.

Competitive Intelligence

Competitive intelligence: data that can be used to improve market share.

Cooperative Strategies

Cooperative strategies are changes made by multiple organizations together.

Defenders

Defenders are companies that maintain one successful product for a long time.

Diversification

Diversification is placement of resources in new and various areas.

Divestiture

Divestiture is a sale of a business by a company.

Domain Selection

Domain selection is using preexisting knowledge to impact a new market.

Environmental Scanning

Environmental scanning is collecting information about effects of business on the land, water, and air.

Flexible Processes

Flexible processes are reforming core processes so as to meet customization demands.

Independent Strategies

Independent strategies are changes made by one organization or department within an organization.

Merger

Merger is a combination of multiple companies.

Prospectors

Prospectors are companies that are always looking to acquire, sell, or cooperate with other businesses.

Smoothing

Smoothing is diminishing extreme fluctuations in demand by offering automatic discounts when sales reach a certain point.

DSST Practice Test

Want to take this practice test in an online interactive format?
Check out the online resources page, which includes interactive practice questions and much more: **mometrix.com/resources719/dsstprsuper**

1. Which of the following roles would a production supervisor most likely NOT assume?

a. Disseminator of information
b. Liaison between staff and upper management
c. Allocator of resources
d. Creator of company mission statement

2. A phone-room supervisor who spends the weekend helping to build a house for Habitat for Humanity is increasing his:

a. Social capital
b. Human capital
c. Expert power
d. Emotional intelligence

3. At the highest level of management, which of the following is true?

a. Technical skills are more important than conceptual skills.
b. Conceptual skills are more important than technical skills.
c. Human skills are less important than technical skills.
d. Human skills are less important than conceptual skills.

4. At a metropolitan newspaper, the copy desk chief responsible for checking the accuracy of headlines written by nonmanagerial copy editors would be considered what level of management?

a. Top level
b. Middle level
c. Frontline
d. None of the above

5. A supervisor who inadvertently omits the word "not" in an email to an employee has committed what kind of communications error?

a. Encoding
b. Decoding
c. Transmission
d. Misinterpretation

6. A manager who is the guest speaker at a Rotary Club luncheon is performing which of the following roles?

a. Liaison
b. Monitor
c. Disseminator
d. Spokesperson

7. Which of the following is NOT included in the Consumer Bill of Rights?

a. The right to seek damages
b. The right to be informed
c. The right to choose
d. The right to safety

8. Management at a coal-fired power plant that sometimes exceeds EPA emissions standards points to its thousands of customers who benefit from reliable, relatively cheap electricity. Whether aware of it or not, plant management is practicing which of the following?

a. Humanistic philosophy
b. Utilitarian philosophy
c. Kaizen
d. A code of ethics

9. Which view of managerial responsibility is generally considered in direct contrast to profit maximization?

a. Corporate social responsibility
b. Ecocentric management
c. Sustainable growth
d. Relativism

10. Which of the following is NOT a provision of the Sarbanes-Oxley Act of 2002?

a. Senior executives are to take individual responsibility for corporate financial reports.
b. A company's CEO must sign the corporate tax return.
c. Standards are set regarding the independence of external auditors.
d. Criminal penalties associated with white-collar crimes and conspiracies are reduced.

11. A supervisor with a case of management myopia would tend to focus on the company's:

a. History
b. Mission statement
c. Short-term profit
d. Long-range strategic planning

12. What channel of communication would be most effective for a supervisor announcing a restructuring of employee schedules?

a. Face-to-face
b. Telephone
c. E-mail
d. Memo

13. The CEO of a grocery chain issues a recall of a certain brand of ground beef after reports of *E. coli* contamination. What kind of decision has he made?

a. Programmed
b. Non-programmed
c. Proactive
d. Reactive

14. A floor supervisor at a garment-manufacturing shop who is able to quickly repair a balky sewing machine is demonstrating which of the following skills?

a. Technical
b. Analytical
c. Technical and analytical
d. Technical and conceptual

15. Of the following kinds of decisions or decision models, which most accurately describes a supervisor's decision to extend the afternoon break so workers may celebrate the birthday of a longtime employee?

a. Political
b. Administrative
c. Rational
d. Intuitive

16. Coaching is a form of:

a. Upward communication
b. Downward communication
c. Horizontal communication
d. Informal communication

17. Human dignity and *kyosei* are two ideals embodied in the set of ethical guidelines known as the:

a. Caux principles
b. Ceres principles
c. ISO 9001
d. WARN Act

18. Life-cycle analysis is used to determine a product's:

a. Shelf life
b. Environmental impact
c. Economic viability
d. Organic structure

19. Which of the following statements does NOT apply to nonverbal communication?

a. It is less powerful than verbal communication.
b. It can occur unintentionally.
c. It is especially important for global companies.
d. It involves skills that can be honed.

20. Which of the following is an example of insider trading?

a. A geologist buys stock in an oil company featured in an issue of Oil & Gas Journal.
b. A chief information officer purchases stock in advance of a merger to be announced the following week.
c. A broker advises her clients to invest in a wind farm after it receives a sizable federal grant.
d. A buyer on E*TRADE purchases stock in an initial public offering.

21. A designer who tells fellow team members that the division intends to cut the team's budget is:

a. Probing
b. Gatekeeping
c. Informing
d. Parading

22. The factory built by Henry Ford to produce the Model T automobile is a classic example of:

a. Systematic management
b. Scientific management
c. Administrative management
d. Quantitative management

23. Which of the following is best suited to a narrow span of control?

a. An assembly line
b. A roomful of telephone survey takers
c. A department-store sales force
d. A research project

24. Which of the following is true of decentralized decision-making?

a. An organization is able to respond rapidly to change.
b. Top-level managers make most of the on-the-spot decisions.
c. Assignments are rarely delegated.
d. Middle-level managers are primarily responsible for innovation.

25. An example of a staff department at Boeing Company would be:

a. Fabrication
b. Product design
c. Assembly
d. Human resources

26. Which of the following would a company consider least when forecasting its internal labor supply?

a. Turnover
b. Terminations
c. Transfers
d. Tardiness

27. According to recent surveys, most job positions are filled through:

a. Newspaper ads
b. Employment agencies
c. Web job boards such as Monster
d. Word of mouth

28. The concept of "employment-at-will" maintains that:

a. A candidate's hiring is contingent upon satisfactory background checks
b. An employee may be terminated for any reason
c. An employee is free to quit at any time
d. A company should offer outplacement to laid-off workers

29. Which of the following statements best applies to external recruiting?

a. It draws from a limited pool of applicants.
b. It infuses "new blood" into an organization.
c. It's an effective way of retaining employees.
d. It tends to rely on a job-posting system.

30. Which of the following is <u>NOT</u> among the five pillars of competitive advantage?

a. Quality
b. Speed
c. Collaboration
d. Service

31. A supervisor conducting a termination interview should:

a. Be as vague as possible to spare the employee's feelings.
b. Hold the interview the day after the employee returns from vacation and is most rested.
c. Let the employee respond at length to the reasons for dismissal.
d. Wrap up the interview within 15 minutes.

32. Generally, the most effective training method for developing management is:

a. Role playing
b. Coaching
c. Job rotation
d. Seminars

33. An employee's initiative would be assessed as part of a supervisor's:

a. Trait appraisal
b. Behavioral appraisal
c. Training appraisal
d. Results appraisal

34. In a 360-degree appraisal, an employee's work is assessed:

a. On a daily basis
b. By subordinates, peers, and superiors
c. By internal and external customers
d. At the completion of a project

35. Generally, a supervisory leader:

a. Anticipates future scenarios
b. Initiates change
c. Provides feedback
d. Creates a vision for the organization

36. A drill sergeant who tells a new recruit to remake his bed is exercising:

a. Legitimate power
b. Reward power
c. Coercive power
d. Referent power

37. A supervisor who exhibits group-maintenance behavior most likely would:

a. Request regular progress reports
b. Show appreciation for a job well done
c. Be a stickler regarding regulations
d. Expect workers to meet deadlines

38. Which of the following scenarios would most likely call for autocratic decision-making?

a. A lead stylist deciding whether to hire a color expert to conduct a seminar for her staff
b. A museum curator deciding how best to install a new exhibit
c. An emergency room doctor deciding which victims of a car crash to treat first
d. A retail manager deciding to wait and see whether to introduce a trendy new line

39. Which of the following statements is true of a leader who has high-maturity followers?

a. Task performance behaviors are more important than group maintenance behaviors.
b. Group maintenance behaviors are more important than task performance behaviors.
c. Both task performance and group maintenance behaviors are important.
d. Both task performance and group maintenance behaviors are relatively unimportant.

40. A supervisor who inspires employees to place the greater good of the organization ahead of their personal interests is a:

a. Transformational leader
b. Transactional leader
c. Charismatic leader
d. Bridge leader

41. A restaurant manager who sends a waitress home without pay for violating the dress code is administering:

a. Positive reinforcement
b. Negative reinforcement
c. Punishment
d. Extinction

42. Which of the following is at the top of Maslow's need hierarchy?

a. Ego
b. Safety
c. Self-actualization
d. Social

43. Which of the following is true?

a. Intrinsic rewards help to motivate creativity.
b. Extrinsic rewards help to motivate creativity.
c. Both intrinsic and extrinsic rewards help to motivate creativity.
d. Neither intrinsic nor extrinsic rewards help to motivate creativity.

44. Which of the following is NOT one of Herzberg's hygiene factors?

a. Coworkers
b. Working conditions
c. Monthly paycheck
d. Using a cash register

45. An organization in which employees are empowered to make decisions would most likely be based on:

a. Bureaucratic control
b. Market control
c. Clan control
d. No control

46. A supervisor tallying absenteeism during the past fiscal year is:

a. Setting a performance standard
b. Measuring performance
c. Comparing performance
d. Correcting performance

47. A plant manager applying the principle of exception would concentrate on:

a. Tires that failed to meet manufacturing standards during a production period
b. Tires that met manufacturing standards during a production period
c. All tires manufactured during a production period
d. Tires to be manufactured during the next production period

48. Preliminary control is the same as which of the following?

a. Feed-forward control
b. Concurrent control
c. Feedback control
d. Bureaucratic control

49. A supervisor in a company undergoing major restructuring who gives a resistant employee a key role in the change process is engaging in:

a. Explicit coercion
b. Implicit coercion
c. Cooptation
d. Negotiation

50. In announcing his decision to add the repair of saddles and horse tack to his shoe-repair business, the owner/manager cites a decline in shoe repair and points to the number of horse properties near the shop's suburban location. In terms of motivating his employees to embrace this change—which will require additional employee training—the owner/manager is at which of the following stages?

a. Unfreezing
b. Moving
c. Refreezing
d. Force-field analysis

51. Which of the following statements is NOT true of organizational development (OD)?

a. It features a behavioral sciences aspect.
b. It focuses on economic and financial aspects of the organization.
c. One of its underlying principles is to support human potential.
d. It supports competitive advantage.

52. Which of the following schools of management thought emphasized greater workforce productivity?

a. Classical management
b. Behavioral management
c. Systems theory
d. Contingency theory

53. Of the following management figures, who could best be described as a universal theorist?

a. Chester Barnard
b. Henri Fayol
c. Elton Mayo
d. Joan Woodward

54. Of the following hiring decisions, which would be most likely to result in the greatest cognitive dissonance?

a. Selecting a chief financial officer from among several highly qualified candidates
b. Selecting a sales representative from several candidates with varying qualifications
c. Selecting a statistician who clearly was the most qualified
d. Selecting a qualified word processor who was the only applicant

55. Which of the following is NOT a component of a SWOT analysis?

a. Strategies
b. Weaknesses
c. Opportunities
d. Threats

56. A sportswear manufacturing company that also owns a textile plant is practicing which of the following strategies?

a. Differentiation
b. Diversification
c. Vertical integration
d. Concentrating on a single business

57. In an ideal organization, which of the following is true?

a. The organizational structure remains constant.
b. The organizational structure supports strategy.
c. The organizational structure dictates strategy.
d. The organizational structure supersedes strategy.

58. Which of the following approaches to job design allows employees the most discretion over their work?

a. Job specialization
b. Job rotation
c. Job enrichment
d. Job enlargement

59. An employee who persists in monopolizing a lunchroom conversation despite ongoing subtle (and not-so-subtle) cues from coworkers is exhibiting low:

a. Self-esteem
b. Self-concept
c. Self-efficacy
d. Self-monitoring

60. The adage "first impressions are lasting impressions" is another way of expressing which of the following perceptual biases?

a. Stereotyping
b. Primacy
c. Recency
d. Halo effect

61. Goal-setting theory maintains which of the following?

a. People who set goals perform better than those who don't.
b. Easy goals lead to higher performance than difficult ones.
c. General goals are more effective than specific ones.
d. Goals assigned by a supervisor are more effective than those designed with employee input.

62. Which of the following is a measure of solvency rather than liquidity?

a. The acid-test ratio
b. Accounts receivable turnover
c. Inventory turnover
d. Ratio of net income (before interest and taxes) to interest expenses

63. Finish the following sentence: A Pareto chart

a. Plots measurements taken over specific intervals
b. Is the same as a bar chart
c. Displays the number of defects in a product over time
d. Shows the relationship between two characteristics or events

64. Which of the following statements is false?

a. Statistical process control (SPC) assumes that every system contains variables.
b. Total quality control (TQC) uses statistics to integrate quality control throughout an organization.
c. SPC assumes that nature is imperfect.
d. TQC assumes that a permanent level of quality can be achieved.

65. Which of the following types of organization would be most likely to have a central marketing department?

a. Functional organization
b. Divisional organization
c. Network organization
d. Dynamic network

66. Which of the following is NOT true of effective followers?

a. They defer to the leader's vision.
b. They wait to be told what to do.
c. They recognize their role in the organization.
d. They seek to increase their skill set.

67. A rubber band manufacturer that uses the Six Sigma approach can expect to produce approximately how many defective rubber bands per million?

a. 5,000
b. 500
c. 50
d. 5

68. Which of the following accurately expresses the relationship among the three elements of a balance sheet?

a. Assets = Liabilities + Stockholders' equity
b. Assets = Liabilities – Stockholders' equity
c. Stockholders' equity = Assets – Liabilities
d. Liabilities = Assets – Stockholders' equity

69. A hardwood flooring company that stockpiles a shipment of Brazilian cherry is doing which of the following?

a. Changing domain
b. Buffering
c. Smoothing
d. Rationing

70. A supervisor who is a proponent of Douglas McGregor's Theory Y would most likely assume that employees:

a. Need external motivation
b. Require constant supervision
c. Want to work
d. Work solely for monetary gain

71. Alderfer developed his ERG theory in response to gaps he perceived in which other theory of motivation?

a. Maslow's hierarchy of needs
b. Herzberg's two-factor theory
c. McClelland's learned needs theory
d. Adams' equity theory

72. In Fiedler's contingency theory, a leader with a low LPC score is likely to have a style that is:

a. More relationship-oriented than task-oriented.
b. More task-oriented than relationship-oriented.
c. Equally task- and relationship-oriented.
d. Dependent on the situation.

73. A temporary team composed of people from different jobs or sections that operates outside the normal structure and is formed to recommend a solution to a specific problem is a:

a. Work team
b. Project and development team
c. Parallel team
d. Management team

74. From management's point of view, the worst group performance occurs in which of the following scenarios?

a. A highly cohesive group with high-performance norms
b. A highly cohesive group with low-performance norms
c. A non-cohesive group with high-performance norms
d. A non-cohesive group with low-performance norms

75. Of the following methods of dealing with conflict, which involves cooperation without assertiveness?

a. Accommodation
b. Avoidance
c. Competing
d. Compromise

76. Which of the following is NOT one of the four primary functions of management?

a. Planning
b. Leading
c. Budgeting
d. Controlling

77. A bookstore manager determining how much space to allot to a new section for gift cards and non-book items is at which stage of the decision-making process?

a. Establishing decision criteria
b. Weighing criteria
c. Developing alternatives
d. Evaluating alternatives

78. Sending questionnaires to experts is part of what decision-making process?

a. Brainstorming
b. Nominal group technique
c. Delphi technique
d. Synergistic effect

79. Who among the following takes the greatest risk when a new technology is introduced to an organization?

a. Change agent
b. Executive champion
c. Product champion
d. Technical innovator

80. Which of the following is NOT true of empowerment?

a. It helps to reduce costs.
b. It requires clear strategic direction.
c. It restricts calculated risk-taking.
d. It allows on-the-spot decisions and action.

81. The Hawthorne Studies led researchers to believe which of the following?

a. Productivity is more greatly influenced by psychological and social factors than by physical working conditions.
b. Productivity is more greatly influenced by working conditions than by psychological and social factors.
c. Productivity is more greatly influenced by working conditions than by economic incentives.
d. Productivity is influenced by economic incentives only.

82. Which of the following laws created the classifications of exempt and non-exempt employees?

a. Fair Labor Standards Act
b. Civil Rights Act
c. Equal Pay Act
d. Age Discrimination in Employment Act

83. During most of the past two decades, the costs of employee benefits have:

a. Risen faster than wages and salaries
b. Risen more slowly than wages and salaries
c. Risen at roughly the same pace as wages and salaries
d. Decreased

84. What percentage of a company's employees must sign authorization cards in order for the National Labor Relations Board to conduct an election on whether workers want to unionize?

a. At least 20 percent
b. At least 30 percent
c. At least 40 percent
d. At least 50 percent

85. Which of the following statements applies to a wildcat strike?

a. It is permitted by law.
b. It also is referred to as an economic strike.
c. It violates the contract between a union and management.
d. It occurs during negotiations before a contract is reached.

86. The Supreme Court decision declaring segregation unconstitutional was:

a. Roe v. Wade.
b. Brown v. Board of Education.
c. Dred Scott v. Sanford
d. NAACP v. Alabama

87. A supervisor who does not participate in sexual harassment but fails to prevent or correct a hostile work environment is:

a. Not liable should a lawsuit be filed
b. Not liable should a lawsuit be filed by a male
c. Liable should a lawsuit be filed
d. Engaging in *quid pro quo* harassment

88. Which adjective best describes a monolithic organization?

a. Heterogeneous
b. Homogeneous
c. Pluralistic
d. Parochial

89. An employee who informs a supervisor that he has AIDS should be:

a. Encouraged to keep working
b. Urged to quit
c. Fired immediately
d. Given indefinite sick leave

90. Which of the following statements is true?

a. Global corporations tend to be based in one country.
b. Multinational companies pursue strategies that differ from country to country.
c. Multinational companies operate as if the world were a single market.
d. Global corporations tend to have their manufacturing facilities in one country.

91. An exchange control is:

a. A limit on the goods that may enter or leave a country
b. A limit on the profit that a company may return to its home country
c. A ban on the import or export of certain products
d. A tax on imported or exported goods

92. A supervisor who is screening job applicants would break the law by asking which of the following questions?

a. Are you authorized to work in the United States?
b. Have you ever been convicted of a felony?
c. Do you have any children?
d. Do you use illegal drugs?

93. Of the external forces that might affect a brewery, which of the following is a direct force?

a. A state law raising the legal drinking age
b. A decline in unemployment rates
c. An increase in wine consumption
d. A supplier of hops

94. Which of the following regulatory agencies would investigate a complaint concerning the private use of a corporate jet by an investment firm's CEO?

a. Federal Aviation Administration
b. Securities and Exchange Commission
c. National Transportation Safety Board
d. Environmental Protection Agency

95. Finish the following sentence: Competition is most intense in industries where:

a. Growth is slow and products are well differentiated.
b. Growth is slow and products are not well differentiated.
c. Growth is rapid and products are well differentiated.
d. Growth is rapid and products are not well differentiated.

96. Which of the following would be the least telling indicator of an organization's culture?

a. Its mission statement
b. Its transportation costs
c. An embellished story about its founder
d. The size of its Christmas bonuses

97. The Maastricht Treaty formally established the:

a. World Trade Organization
b. Asia-Pacific Economic Cooperative
c. European Union
d. North American Free Trade Agreement

98. Which of the following is NOT a factor in the decline of US manufacturing jobs?

a. Outsourcing
b. Insourcing
c. Offshoring
d. Innovation

99. Loss of control over quality is a drawback associated with which of the following ways to enter overseas markets?

a. Exporting
b. Licensing
c. Franchising
d. Joint ventures

100. Which of the following workers' age groups is projected to be the fastest-growing in the decade from 2004 to 2014?

a. 16 to 24
b. 25 to 34
c. 35 to 44
d. 55 and older

Answer Key and Explanations

1. D: Creator of company mission statement. A link between workers and management, a production supervisor is a frontline manager whose tasks most likely include conveying information and acting as a liaison between workers and upper management. A production supervisor also may be responsible for the direct allocation of certain resources or materials needed by workers to do their jobs. However, top-level management is responsible for a company's overarching vision and goals, so a company's mission statement would be created by senior executives, perhaps with the aid of a staff writer or PR person, and *not* by a production supervisor.

2. A: Social capital. Social capital is the goodwill that results from social relationships, whether personal or online at sites such as Facebook or LinkedIn. *Spending a weekend building a house through Habitat for Humanity would be one way to build social capital.* Human capital is the economic or strategic value of employees' knowledge and abilities, while a leader with obvious knowledge and abilities is said to have expert power. Expert power induces people to comply because they believe they can learn or benefit from that expertise. Emotional intelligence, or EQ, is the set of skills that allows a person to know and manage himself and deal effectively with others. Although a supervisor who helps to build a house for Habitat for Humanity might well have a high degree of emotional intelligence and empathy for others, a weekend of volunteering would increase his social capital—and, most likely, that of his company.

3. B: Conceptual skills are more important than technical skills. Although successful managers are able to call upon a variety of skills, different levels of management emphasize different skill sets. Technical skills and the ability to perform assigned tasks are most important for nonmanagerial employees and frontline supervisors. As one rises in the management hierarchy, the ability to think broadly and make strategic decisions becomes more important; *conceptual skills become more important than technical skills.* Good people skills are important at every level.

4. C: Frontline. Top-level managers, or senior executives, are strategic managers who tend to focus on the big picture, outlining a company's goals and vision. Middle-level managers bridge the gap between the two, conveying the goals of top management to lower-level management and relaying operational information and concerns to upper management. A supervisor who oversees the day-to-day work of non-management employees, as in this scenario, would be a frontline manager.

5. A: Encoding. In one-way communication, a sender encodes the information he wishes to convey into symbols, or words, which are then transmitted via a written, oral, or electronic channel to a receiver, who decodes and interprets the message. Errors can occur at all stages of communication. *Encoding errors* may include misused or ambiguous words and phrases and misstatement of fact. Transmission errors include lost or misplaced mail or a soft voice that's difficult to hear. Decoding problems include misreading or not listening carefully. Misinterpretation may include jumping to a wrong conclusion or taking a humorous remark seriously. Communication problems are less apt to occur in two-way communication, which is when, after decoding and interpreting the information, the receiver provides feedback to the sender. In true two-way communication, the original sender is receptive to feedback, and this give-and-take helps to clarify the message.

6. D: Spokesperson. According to a study by Henry Mintzberg, managers fulfill 10 roles that fall into three basic categories: interpersonal, which includes the roles of figurehead, liaison, and leadership; informational, which includes the roles of monitor, disseminator, and spokesperson; and decisional, which includes the roles of entrepreneur, resource allocator, disturbance handler, and negotiator. When a manager represents the views of his department or organization—whether inside or outside the organization—that manager is acting in the informational role of spokesperson.

7. A: The right to seek damages. The Consumer Bill of Rights was enacted by President Kennedy in the 1960s and established four basic rights of the consumer. The right to safety means that consumers should be able to rely on the safety of the products they buy and use. The right to be informed means that consumers can receive information about a product before they buy it. The right to choose means that consumers can select from an array of competitively priced products. The right to be heard means that consumers can voice their opinion regarding policies and decisions that affect them. Although consumers certainly have the right to seek damages—and often do so in such cases as wrongful death or class action lawsuits—that right is separate from the Consumer Bill of Rights and is, therefore, *not* one of the four basic rights it establishes.

8. B: Utilitarian philosophy. Proponents of humanistic philosophy focus on the rights and values of individuals—customers and workers alike. Those who follow utilitarian philosophy espouse the greatest good for the greatest number, even if a product or process is flawed. The Japanese word "kaizen" (and its philosophy) emphasizes the continual improvement of an organization, as well as one's life. A code of ethics is a set of written guidelines spelling out ethical behavior according to an organization's values and standards. Managers for the plant in this problem are aware of a flaw in their process but justify it by pointing to a "greater" benefit. As such, they are obviously practicing a utilitarian philosophy.

9. A: Corporate social responsibility. Profit maximization—a tenet of capitalism espoused by Adam Smith and, later, Milton Friedman—maintains that the primary responsibility of managers is to increase the value of the company and thus increase profits for shareholders, on whose behalf they act. That view traditionally has been most at odds with corporate social responsibility, which maintains that business has an obligation toward society and should assume responsibility for the impact of its activities. However, companies today are realizing that behaving in a socially responsible manner need not preclude profitability. Ecocentric management (which seeks to benefit society worldwide by maximizing sustainable economic development) and sustainable growth (economic growth that meets current needs while preserving the environment so that future needs can be met) are examples of corporate environmental management, which offers increasing advantages and opportunities in today's "green-conscious" world. Relativism is a moral philosophy which maintains that truth and values are relative rather than absolute and are based on the opinions and actions of others. "Everybody else cheats on their income taxes. Why shouldn't I?" is an example of moral relativism.

10. D: Criminal penalties associated with white-collar crimes and conspiracies are reduced. The Sarbanes-Oxley Act of 2002—enacted in response to outrage over the scandals involving Enron, WorldCom, Adelphia, and other major corporations—established new or enhanced federal standards for the boards and management of publicly held US companies and accounting firms. The legislation does not apply to privately held companies. In general, the act seeks to make management and auditors more financially accountable and thus bolster investor confidence. Among the act's provisions, senior executives must personally sign off on company financial reports, and the CEO must sign the corporate tax return. Standards are set regarding the independence of auditors as well as the independence of boards of directors, which are not to consist solely of company insiders. Penalties—including fines and criminal prosecution—for white-collar crimes are *increased*, not reduced. Therefore, D is the correct answer.

11. C: Short-term profit. Management myopia is when management focuses on the short range outcomes, rather than take the longer, strategic view. Management myopia often is caused by financial ratios, which are expressed in short-term increments such as months, quarters, or a year, and which encourage managers to emphasize short-term profits and earnings. Conversely, an organization's history, mission statement, and long-range strategic planning require managers to be far-sighted, not short-sighted.

12. A: Face-to-face. In general, difficult or unusual information should be conveyed through "media rich" channels, or those that convey the most information. Face-to-face generally is considered the most media rich way to communicate because it provides the greatest number of cues and feedback. As communication becomes less personal, it becomes less media rich; thus a memo is the least media rich way to communicate. Less media rich channels are better suited for routine messages that don't require a response. Because a restructuring of employee schedules would most likely be an unusual and possibly upsetting scenario, the most effective way to announce the decision would be at a face-to-face meeting with employees, giving them an opportunity to ask questions and voice concerns.

13. D: Reactive. Programmed decisions are made in situations that are routine and repetitive, and the rules for making such decisions are well established. Such decisions are cut and dried, as opposed to non-programmed decisions, which are customized for unstructured or unique situations that call for creative alternatives. Proactive decisions are those made in advance of changing environments or situations and can prevent future problems. Reactive decisions—as in the case of this ground beef recall—are those made in response to changing environments or situations, and often are an attempt to put out a fire.

14. A: Technical. Technical skills are the specialized knowledge and proficiencies needed to perform specific tasks. Front-line managers especially use technical skills to solve daily problems and manage production, much as this floor supervisor who repairs the defective sewing machine. Analytical skills involve the ability to logically analyze and solve complex problems, often with the aid of computer software. Middle management uses analytical techniques such as projections or forecasts to aid in decision-making. Conceptual skills are the ability to consider abstract ideas and the relationships among them and thus see the big picture. Top management uses conceptual skills when considering the organization and its goals as a whole, as well as its various components and how they work together to achieve the organization's objectives. Although a floor supervisor may use some analytical skills to determine why a machine isn't working, such skills would be part of his technical expertise and not the highly analytical and logical skills required to solve complex problems.

15. A: Political. In the political model, decisions are non-programmed—that is, not routine or repetitive. Politically based decisions are not necessarily the best decisions but are those most acceptable to the group. The decision to extend break in order to celebrate a long-time employee's birthday falls into this category. The administrative model assumes that people never have enough information to make the ultimate best decision, and even if they had such information, they'd be unable to completely process it. The administrative model seeks a satisfactory decision; the first acceptable decision available will suffice. In such a model, decisions may be programmed or non-programmed. The rational model is based on logic and facts, and assumes an optimal decision is possible. Considered somewhat simplistic, the rational model works when choices are clear-cut and decisions are programmed. Although intuitive decisions are based on gut feelings or beliefs, they are not necessarily irrational but may be the result of knowledge and experience that allow a flash of insight or intuition.

16. B: Downward communication. Upward communication is the flow of information from lower to higher levels of management. Downward communication is the flow of information from upper to lower management, and horizontal communication is the flow of information across the same level of management. Informal communication is not official communication at all and includes gossip, personal emails, and lunchroom conversations—all the elements that make up the informal social network of communication called the grapevine. Coaching is a dialogue in which a manager gives feedback to someone who reports directly to him, with the intent of developing the person's potential or improving performance. Because of that, it would be considered an example of downward communication.

17. A: Caux principles. The Caux Round Table (CRT) describes itself as an international network of principled business leaders working to promote a moral capitalism. In 1994 it established the Caux principles, described as a worldwide vision for ethical and responsible corporate behavior. This "statement of aspirations" is rooted in two basic ideals: *kyosei* and human dignity. According to the CRT, the Japanese concept of *kyosei* means living and working together for the common good, enabling cooperation and mutual prosperity to coexist with healthy and fair competition. By "human dignity," the CRT means the sacredness or value of each person as an end, not simply as a means to the fulfillment of others' purposes or even majority goals. The Ceres principles is a 10-point code of corporate environmental conduct proposed by Ceres; a nonprofit group formed shortly after the Exxon-Valdez oil spill in 1989. In 1993, Sunoco became the first Fortune 500 company to endorse the Ceres principles; since then, more than 50 companies have followed suit. The 10 principles include protection of the biosphere, sustainable use of natural resources, and safe and responsible reduction and disposal of wastes. ISO 9001 is a voluntary standard developed by the International Organization for Standardization (ISO) that applies in a general way to management systems. ISO 9001 doesn't guarantee the specific quality of products or services but assures that formalized business processes have been applied. The Worker Adjustment and Retraining Notification (WARN) Act requires employers to provide 60 days' notice of plant closings and mass layoffs, as long as certain conditions apply.

18. B: Environmental impact: Life-cycle analysis, also known as "cradle-to-grave analysis," is the process of determining a product's total environmental impact—from its manufacture to end use to disposal. Companies increasingly are realizing that corporate environmental responsibility need not preclude profit and are beginning to assess the impacts of production—especially when alternatives are available. Shelf life is the length of time a product can remain on a retailer's shelf without becoming unsuitable for use. Economic viability is the capability of an enterprise to survive and grow; profitability is a measure of economic viability. Organic structure (in the business rather than biological sense) refers to an organizational structure that is fluid, flexible, and much less rigid than traditional, hierarchical structures.

19. A: It is less powerful than verbal communication. Nonverbal communication is *not* less powerful than verbal communication. In business, as in life, actions often speak louder than words. The contractor who won't look you in the eye, the seat of honor at a conference, a supplier who is chronically late—all are signals that can strengthen, dilute, or negate the verbal messages being conveyed. When conducting business in foreign countries, where verbal communication may be sketchy at best, nonverbal communication assumes added importance. Business deals can be lost simply because nonverbal cues were misinterpreted. Many of the gestures and nonverbal messages we take for granted in the United States mean something entirely different abroad. In Bulgaria, for instance, nodding the head means "no" rather than "yes." It's important to be aware of body language and facial expressions—which research suggests may comprise up to 90 percent of communication between people—as well as the impact of seating arrangements and office layout.

Time is another nonverbal consideration. A manager who constantly looks at his watch while meeting with an employee—or who doesn't have time to meet at all—is sending a message, whether he knows it or not.

20. B: A chief information officer purchases stock in advance of a merger to be announced the following week. According to the Securities and Exchange Commission (SEC), insider trading actually includes both legal and illegal conduct. It's legal for corporate insiders—officers, directors, and employees—to buy and sell stock in their own companies. However, they must report those trades to the SEC. Illegal insider trading generally refers to buying or selling a security while having substantive, nonpublic information about it. The SEC also considers "tipping" such information illegal, as is securities trading by the person "tipped" and securities trading by those who misappropriate such information. Examples of SEC insider trading cases are those involving corporate officers, directors, and employees who traded the corporation's securities after learning of significant, confidential corporate developments; friends, associates, family members, and other "tippees" of such insiders who traded the securities after receiving such information, and employees of law, banking, brokerage and printing firms who were given such information in order to provide services to the corporation whose securities they then traded.

21. B: Gatekeeping. Teams are not insulated but must interact with others inside and outside the organization. Probing is a strategy that requires team members to focus on external relationships, diagnose needs (of customers, for example), and experiment with solutions. Gatekeeping is when a team member relays relevant information—from within or outside the organization—to the rest of the team, as in this case. Informing is when outsiders are told about a team decision. Parading is when a team seeks to strengthen itself internally while enhancing external visibility.

22. B: Scientific management. Management theory and practices have been evolving since the Industrial Revolution and continue to do so. In the late 19th century, systematic management raised awareness of the managerial process, emphasizing standardization, coordination, and organizational control to meet burgeoning consumer demand. But unrealized production efficiency led Frederick Taylor, a young engineer, to introduce the concept of scientific management, which used scientific methods such as time/motion studies to determine the most efficient way to perform a task. Taylor also emphasized the importance of training, standardized tools, and instruction cards to help workers do the best possible job. Henry Ford's innovative, moving production line that allowed automobiles to be efficiently assembled by specialized workers in sequence is an example of scientific management in practice. Administrative management maintained that management was a profession that could be taught, and Henri Fayol, another engineer, developed 14 principles of management. Quantitative management is a more contemporary approach, using mathematical models and quantitative analysis to solve management problems.

23. D: A research project. Span of control refers to the number of people who report directly to a supervisor. A narrow span of control, with few people reporting directly to a single supervisor, tends to create a vertical or "tall" organization with many layers of management. A wide span of control, with many people reporting directly to a supervisor, builds a horizontal or "flat" organization with fewer managers. Factors that may affect span of control include job complexity, similarity of jobs, physical proximity of employees to manager, and the abilities of employees and manager. In general, the span should be narrower when the work is complex or ambiguous, the subordinates' jobs are disparate and non-routine, the manager is remote or non-supportive, jobs lack common performance standards, or workers need or prefer close supervision. Because research is more complex and non-routine than assembly, retail sales, or survey-taking, with job performance far less standardized and thus difficult to quantify, it is well suited to a narrow span of control. In general, a research project manager would be able to effectively manage fewer people than an assembly, sales, or survey supervisor.

24. A: An organization is able to respond rapidly to change. A decentralized organization is one in which authority has been delegated throughout different levels of management, while a centralized organization is one in which authority is concentrated at the top levels of management. Because decision-making can occur quickly at the point of implementation, a decentralized organization is able to respond to change more rapidly than a centralized organization that must relay information to top management and await its decision. Ideally, innovation is encouraged at all levels of management, whether an organization is centralized or decentralized.

25. D: Human resources. Line departments are directly engaged in the production, sales, or service of a company's products. Fabrication, product design, assembly, distribution, and customer service are examples of line departments. Staff departments, on the other hand, are specialized units of professionals who support line departments. They often wield considerable power and include legal, research, accounting, public relations, and human resources departments.

26. D: Tardiness. Supply of labor—the number and kinds of employees available to an organization—consists of two primary components: external, which is labor supply outside the company, and internal, which is labor supply within the company. To forecast external supply, an organization must consider workforce trends, both nationally and globally. When forecasting its internal supply, an organization considers turnover, terminations, transfers, promotions, and retirement. Although chronic tardiness may affect production and ultimately lead to termination, it would *not* be an important consideration when forecasting an organization's labor supply.

27. D: Word of mouth. Web job boards, such as Monster, are booming in popularity, and newspaper ads are experiencing resurgence as a result of partnering with those online job boards. Employment agencies and headhunters are especially popular with companies seeking to fill top-level positions. But nothing beats word of mouth. According to a 2006 article in *Workforce Management,* surveys show that most jobs are filled by word-of-mouth referrals. Not only is it an inexpensive way to recruit, but current employees have the inside track on knowing who will be a good fit with their company.

28. B: An employee may be terminated for any reason. Employment-at-will, also known as termination-at-will, is the concept that a company may fire an employee for any reason. There are, of course, exceptions to this policy, and courts have been actively involved in defining those exceptions for many years. But the concept itself has been on the legal books since the 19th century and is a logical parallel to the fact that an employee may quit whenever he wishes. Although a candidate's hiring often is contingent upon reference or background checks, those have nothing to do with employment-at-will. Neither does the arguably moral obligation to offer outplacement to laid-off workers.

29. B: It infuses "new blood" into an organization. External recruiting is when an organization seeks to hire candidates from outside the company. By hiring outside the company, an organization effectively gains "new blood." External recruiting, which draws from a much broader pool of applicants, brings in candidates who are not immersed in the organization's culture and procedures. Conversely, internal recruiting is when an organization hires or promotes from within. While internal recruiting may provide an incentive for employees to stay with a company, the organization's pool of candidates is then effectively limited by the number of existing employees who can perform the proposed job. Job postings—on bulletin boards, employee newsletters and the like—are a common way for companies to recruit internally.

30. C: Collaboration. The five pillars that help an organization gain and maintain its competitive edge are speed, cost, quality, innovation, and service. Successful organizations focus on all five types of performance. Skimping on even one can undercut a company's competitive edge. Although collaboration within an organization—and even between competitors in the global marketplace—is playing an increasingly important role in business today, it is not considered one of the five pillars of performance upon which an organization builds a competitive advantage.

31. D: Wrap up the interview within 15 minutes. Ideally, an employee is terminated only after receiving progressive warnings or disciplinary measures and the opportunity to correct his shortcomings. The hallmarks of a termination interview are professionalism and courtesy. The employee should be told in a succinct, direct manner that he is being terminated, and why. The supervisor should not be drawn into a debate or discussion of the matter, and the interview should take no more than 15 minutes. It is, at best, insensitive to fire an employee on his birthday or any significant anniversary. Neither should he be fired when on vacation or immediately after such.

32. B: Coaching. Management training programs are designed to increase managers' effectiveness in dealing with others. Although role-playing, job rotation, and seminars or courses are useful tools for supervisors, as well as other employees, coaching generally is considered the most effective way to develop management. Similar to an apprenticeship, a coaching or mentoring program allows a supervisor to observe the day-to-day issues and decisions faced by a more experienced manager, who in turn is able to observe, instruct and—if necessary—correct the supervisor in a variety of situations.

33. A: Trait appraisal. Training generally refers to teaching an employee how to do a job, whereas appraisals evaluate how well the job is being performed. Traits, behaviors, and results comprise the three basic categories of performance appraisal. A trait appraisal, which rates certain employee characteristics pertaining to job performance, is quite subjective and can be misleading. For instance, an employee who seems aloof might simply be reserved. Behavioral appraisals are somewhat more objective and measure observable actions or behaviors. An employee might routinely make excuses for not meeting deadlines, for example. Results appraisals are the most objective of the three, being based on quantifiable data such as sales volume or production. Initiative itself is a trait, meaning it would be evaluated as part of a trait appraisal. It could, however, also lead to a behavior (taking work home to get the job done), thus leading to results (increased sales).

34. B: By subordinates, peers, and superiors. Although employee performance generally is evaluated by supervisors, companies increasingly are seeking input from other sources. Internal customers—that is, other workers within the company who rely on an employee's work or output—and external customers outside the organization might be asked for feedback regarding an employee's performance. A 360-degree appraisal is when an employee's superiors, peers, and subordinates evaluate performance, which helps to provide a well-rounded assessment. It is worth noting that although an employee might be informally judged or evaluated on a daily basis, a formal appraisal is far less frequent and might occur at the completion of a project or at specified time(s) throughout the year.

35. C: Provides feedback. Some people consider the distinction between management and leadership artificial, if not belittling to management, and so prefer to draw a distinction between supervisory and strategic leadership. Supervisory leaders deal with issues affecting the day-to-day operations of an organization. They monitor, guide, and provide feedback and support to their employees, as in this question. Strategic leaders go beyond basic management processes to create a vision for the organization and inspire people to achieve it. They think forward to the future and initiate change, so the organization can effectively meet the envisioned future. It is not impossible for a manager to be both a supervisory and strategic leader.

36. A: Legitimate power. J.R.P. French and B. Raven proposed "The Bases of Social Power" in 1959, and their theory is still widely held today. According to French and Raven, an organization contains five potential sources of power: legitimate power, or authority; reward power, or control over rewards such as pay raises; coercive power, or control over punishments such as docked pay; referent power, which is based on appealing personal characteristics that compel people to comply; and expert power, which is expertise or knowledge that causes people to comply.

A drill sergeant might have some control over rewards and punishments—and might be charismatic and knowledgeable to boot—but when giving an order to a new recruit, he is exercising his legitimate power or authority.

37. B: Show appreciation for a job well done. Traditionally, the study of leadership falls into three categories: the trait approach, the behavioral approach, and the situational approach. The trait approach attempts to single out the personality traits and characteristics shared by great leaders, while the behavioral approach focuses on their behavior—that is, what they do as leaders. The situational approach maintains that great leaders do not necessarily share similar traits or behaviors but that their responses vary depending on the situation. The behavioral approach is further divided into three categories of behaviors: task performance, group maintenance, and employee participation in decision making. Task- performance behaviors are those that focus on getting the job done, emphasizing speed, quality, production, and following the rules. Participation in decision-making examines to what degree a leader lets employees influence decisions. Group-maintenance behaviors focus on relationships and seek to build stable groups that work well together. A supervisor who exhibits group-maintenance behavior, therefore, would be highly likely to show appreciation for a job well done.

38. C: An emergency room doctor deciding which victims of a car crash to treat first. One facet of leadership is the degree to which subordinates are involved in decision making. An autocratic leader is one who makes decisions entirely on his own and then informs employees of that decision. A democratic leader considers employee input before making decisions. A laissez-faire leader, essentially, makes no decision. Each style of leadership has its advantages and drawbacks. By its very nature, the democratic approach results in a more considered, but more time-consuming, decision, while autocratic decision making generally is most appropriate when decisiveness or speed is called for. Both the lead stylist and museum curator easily could—and possibly should—involve subordinates in the decision process. The retail manager who decides to wait and see is taking a laissez-faire approach. The ER doctor, however, has a responsibility to act quickly and decisively in a potentially life-threatening situation and so must use an autocratic decision-making process.

39. D: Both task performance and group maintenance behaviors are relatively unimportant. In Hersey and Blanchard's situational theory (originally called the "life-cycle theory of leadership"), the maturity of the followers helps to determine whether a leader focuses on task-performance or group-maintenance behaviors. High-maturity followers are those who have high levels of job maturity—the technical skills and knowledge to perform a task—as well as high levels of psychological maturity, that is, self-respect and self-confidence. According to this theory, high-maturity followers are able to do a good job regardless of whether a leader exhibits task-performance or group-maintenance behaviors, meaning they are both relatively unimportant.

40. A: Transformational leader. Transformational leaders generate excitement and motivate people to act for the greater good rather than personal interests. Charismatic leaders are dominant, dynamic personalities with strong emotional appeal who, like transformational leaders, generate excitement in their followers. However, charisma is but one quality of the transformational leader, who pays attention to people as individuals and stimulates them both intellectually and emotionally. Transactional leaders are more traditional, emphasizing the transaction—or simple exchange—of reward for effort. They rely on their authority to issue commands and mete out rewards. Bridge leaders are those who leave home to study, work, or travel in another culture. When they return home, the knowledge and insights they have gained allow them to bridge conflicting cultures and values.

41. C: Punishment. Reinforcement theory, which is based on Edward Thorndike's law of effect, considers the relationship between behavior and consequences. When applied in an organization, reinforcement theory is known as organizational behavior modification, or OB mod, which seeks to affect performance through four consequences: positive reinforcement, negative reinforcement, punishment, and extinction. Positive reinforcement is when desirable behavior is rewarded, with the intent of increasing the likelihood that such behavior will be repeated. Negative reinforcement, or avoidance, is when an undesirable consequence is removed or withheld as long as an employee does not behave improperly. Punishment provides a penalty for undesirable behavior, with the intent of decreasing the likelihood that such behavior will be repeated. A waitress being sent home without pay for violation of dress code, as in this problem, is receiving punishment. (Note: The *threat* of punishment is considered negative reinforcement, not punishment.) Extinction is when no consequence or reinforcement—positive or negative—is provided, thus eliminating the behavior.

42. C: Self-actualization. Abraham Maslow developed his need hierarchy as a result of his belief that people satisfy their needs in a specific order. Ascending from bottom to top, Maslow conceived his need hierarchy as: physiological (e.g., food, shelter), safety (or security), social (e.g. friendship, love), ego (e.g. independence, self-esteem), and self-actualization (fulfilling one's potential). Maslow proposed that people are motivated to satisfy their lower needs first. Then when a need is satisfied, it becomes a less powerful motivator.

43. A: Intrinsic rewards help to motivate creativity. Extrinsic rewards come from outside oneself—from a supervisor, an organization, and such. Paychecks, benefits, and appreciation are examples of extrinsic rewards. Intrinsic rewards are inherent in the job itself and the enjoyment of performing it well. A challenging project, a tough deadline met, or problem solved are examples of intrinsic rewards. Not only do intrinsic rewards inspire people to put forth effort above and beyond routine demands, but they are essential in tapping into underlying creativity.

44. D: Using a cash register. In his two-factor theory, Frederick Herzberg proposed that people are affected on the job by two main categories: hygiene factors and motivators. Hygiene factors are characteristics of the workplace, including pay, supervisors, coworkers, working conditions, and the like. Motivators are characteristics of the job, including job responsibilities, potential for advancement, and the work itself. Although scholars tend to discount Herzberg's theory, it played an important role in the development of job design.

45. C: Clan control. William Ouchi of UCLA proposed three basic strategies for controlling organizations: bureaucratic, market, and clan control. Bureaucratic control relies on authoritarian rules and regulations; market control is based on economic data, pricing, and competition; and clan control, which assumes that the organization and the individual have common interests, is based on the shared goals and values of the group. According to Ouchi, clan control works best when employees are empowered to make decisions. "No control" is not a valid option for an organization, which must have some form of control or way to direct its members in order to achieve its goals.

46. B: Measuring performance. A bureaucratic system typically has four key steps. First, it sets a performance standard, then performance is measured, compared and, if necessary, corrected. A performance standard is the expected level of performance for an organizational goal such as profitability, production, sales, and the like. Performance can be measured in money earned, number of items manufactured or sold, repeat customers, and so on. Managers then compare actual performance with the performance standard. If performance deviates too far from the standard, corrective action may be taken. A performance standard might be to reduce absenteeism to 5 percent in a fiscal year. A supervisor would collect data—time sheets, for example—to measure the rate of absenteeism and would then compare that rate with the 5 percent standard. If the rate of absenteeism were 15 percent, for example, corrective action (improving working conditions, instituting an attendance policy, etc.) could be taken.

47. A: Tires that failed to meet manufacturing standards during a production period. The principle of exception states that a manager or evaluator should be concerned with exceptions to or deviations from expected results or standards rather than focus on results that meet or approximate the standard. Results that fail to meet the standard are analyzed in order to correct a problem, whereas results that exceed the standard may be studied to determine how to duplicate such results. Focusing on the exceptions is a much more efficient use of a manager's time and energy.

48. A: Feedforward control. Feedforward, concurrent, and feedback controls are three forms of bureaucratic control. Feedforward controls, also known as preliminary controls, are rules and policies in place before a process begins. Concurrent controls are used while plans are being carried out, and are designed to monitor and direct activities as they occur. Feedback controls involve reviewing performance to make any necessary corrections in the process.

49. C: Cooptation. Employees, like people in general, tend to resist change. Not only do managers often underestimate the resistance they may face, but they underestimate the effectiveness of ways to counter it. Coercion uses threats and punishment to force resistant employees to accept change. In explicit coercion, the negative consequences or punishment are clearly spelled out: "Anyone who doesn't go along with these changes will be fired." In implicit coercion, the punishment may be veiled, but clear nonetheless: "It's obvious that those who resist these changes don't share our company values." Coercion is a highly effective but dangerous strategy that can create hostility among employees and should be used only when speed is of the essence. Cooptation, however, takes place when a resistant employee—often a vocal leader of those opposing change—is given a key role in the change process, as in this example. Cooptation is a form of manipulation, and the "key role" may be symbolic only. The danger here is that the employee may realize he has been manipulated and become even more resistant. Negotiation happens when an employee is offered some reward or concession for cooperating with change. Although a relatively equitable way to manage resistance, negotiation can be expensive, depending on the rewards (bonuses, pay raises, etc.).

50. A: Unfreezing. Unfreezing, moving, and refreezing are the three basic stages of motivating people to change, according to a model developed by Kurt Lewin. In unfreezing, management helps employees realize that past ways of doing things no longer are effective and must be changed, as with the owner-manager of this shoe-repair business. In moving, the actual change is instituted. In refreezing, behavior that supports the change is reinforced. Force-field analysis—a technique also developed by Lewin that helps to manage the change process—identifies forces that cause people to resist change (restraining forces) and those that move people toward change (driving forces).

51. B: It (does NOT) focus on economic and financial aspects of the organization. Organizational development (OD) is a change process that uses behavioral science techniques to systematically improve an organization's effectiveness. Rather than focus directly on technology, operations, or finances, OD takes a broad approach to change employee attitudes and organizational culture. An underlying principle of OD is the support of human development and potential, along with competitive advantage in an ever-changing external environment. Although he died before OD became widely accepted, Kurt Lewin is considered the father of organizational development, as well as the developer of force-field analysis and the freezing/moving/unfreezing model.

52. A: Classical management. Classical management, which includes scientific management and classical organization theory, focuses on greater workforce productivity. It was developed at the beginning of the 20th century when skilled labor was in short supply and organizations sought the most efficient use of available workers. By the mid-20th century, however, it was clear that total worker efficiency was not practicable. Behavioral management, which includes the human relations approach and the behavioral science approach, shifted the focus from employees as efficient "machines" to employees as people, with needs and interactions. In systems theory, the organization is seen as an interrelated whole, in which what happens to one part of the system affects the rest of the system. Contingency theory, unlike classical management, recognizes that there's no "one best way" to manage an organization but that changing technology and environments—internal and external—create different situations that managers must evaluate before deciding the most appropriate course of action.

53. B: Henri Fayol: Universal theorists maintained that there is "one best way" to manage and get work done efficiently, and that certain principles and rules apply in all situations. Situational theorists, on the other hand, believe that—because each situation is different—there is no one best way that applies across the board. Barnard (a pioneer of systems theory), Mayo (behavioral theory), and Woodward (contingency theory) would all be considered situational theorists. Fayol, on the other hand, is a classical theorist who—like Frederick Taylor and Max Weber—believed in universal principles. Not only did Fayol propose 14 principles of management—many of which are pertinent today—but he was the first to consider the four basic management functions: planning, organizing, commanding (leading), and controlling.

54. A: Selecting a chief financial officer from among several highly qualified candidates. Cognitive dissonance is a psychological term that refers to the anxiety or discomfort caused by holding contradictory beliefs, ideas, or attitudes at the same time. In terms of management, cognitive dissonance may occur after a decision has been made if the decision maker perceives a conflict between what he believes and the results of the decision. Cognitive dissonance is similar to buyer's remorse or second-guessing and is a common phenomenon across all levels of management. The more important the decision, the greater the likelihood of a high degree of cognitive dissonance. Cognitive dissonance also may be increased if several alternatives were available and discarded, and if those alternatives had many attractive features—as when selecting new personnel from among several highly qualified candidates.

55. A: Strategies: SWOT is an acronym for strengths, weaknesses, opportunities and threats—factors an organization considers when assessing its current situation as a precursor to strategic change. Strengths and weaknesses are internal factors that include a company's financial and human resources. Opportunities and threats are external and include events with the potential to benefit or harm the company, such as a change in federal regulations or an increasingly saturated market. Although a careful SWOT analysis is beneficial prior to formulating a strategic plan, "strategies" are not themselves part of the SWOT analysis.

56. C: Vertical integration: In differentiation, a business seeks to separate itself from its competition by increasing the perceived value of its products through higher cost and value-added features. Diversification is a corporate strategy in which an organization seeks increased profitability by competing in more than one industry. Diversification may be related (when the different industries or products are similar) or unrelated (when the industries or goods are dissimilar). Vertical integration occurs when a corporation owns or merges with firms that are in its supply chain—as when a sportswear manufacturing company produces its own textiles. Backward integration is when an organization controls all or part of the supply chain that precedes production—raw materials, for example. Forward integration is when the organization controls the supply chain beyond production—for example, distribution. Vertical integration is most cost-efficient and feasible in industries with few stages of production. Concentrating on a single business is just that: when a corporation limits its scope and focuses on one business only.

57. B: The organizational structure supports strategy. Organizational structure is the form or framework an organization uses to direct its people to achieve its objectives and carry out its predefined strategy. An organization's structure is apparent in the way its divisions, departments, and jobs are arranged and interact. Strategy precedes—and, ideally, determines—structure, which should support the organization's overall strategy. Structure often is depicted in a chart. However, structure is not set in stone. The most successful organizations are those that can modify structure to adapt to—or in advance of—changing environments. Weak organizations are those that attempt to modify their strategy to fit an existing structure.

58. C: Job enrichment. Job specialization involves breaking a job into its components, including what tasks are to be performed, in what manner, and how quickly. Job range is the number of tasks a worker performs; job depth is the amount of discretion a worker has in performing tasks. Job rotation is when a number of employees are moved from job to job, increasing the job range of each employee. Job enlargement is an increase in the number of tasks involved in a job, with the intent of lessening worker boredom and dissatisfaction. Job enrichment seeks to give employees greater control over their jobs—and thus greater self-fulfillment—by increasing not only job range but job depth by allowing workers more responsibility and discretion.

59. D: Self-monitoring. A supervisor must be attuned to employees' individual differences, which begin with the notion of self. Self-concept is a person's self-image—the way one sees oneself—and involves accumulated knowledge about oneself, including one's beliefs, attitudes, abilities, etc. Self-esteem is, broadly, the tendency to view the self favorably or unfavorably and is considered the evaluative aspect of self-concept. Self-efficacy, while similar to self-esteem, is situation-specific and is the belief that one can succeed in a particular situation. Self-monitoring is the ability to adjust one's behavior based on sensitivity to others and the cues they provide. An employee who persists in monopolizing lunchroom conversation despite ongoing cues from other workers is exhibiting low self-monitoring.

60. B: Primacy. Supervisors need to be aware of perceptual biases so they can lessen their impact in the workplace. There are several types of perceptual biases. Stereotyping is the process of ascribing to an individual certain exaggerated or simplified characteristics associated with a class or group. Priming, or primacy, is the tendency to give the most weight to initial information or impressions, whereas recency is the tendency to consider the latest information or impressions the most important. Halo effect is the tendency to focus on a particular characteristic, whether negative or positive, and to filter subsequent information about a person on the basis of that characteristic. The old adage about "first impressions" makes reference to the perceptual bias of primacy.

61. A: People who set goals perform better than those who don't. Managers may use goal-setting as a tool to increase employee motivation and productivity. Goal-setting theory maintains that people who set goals perform better than people who don't. In general, difficult—but attainable—goals are more effective than easy ones, and specific goals ("Let's gain five new accounts this month") are more effective than generalities ("Let's beat the competition!"). An important aspect of goal-setting theory is employee acceptance of the goal as his own aspiration. Thus, employee involvement in goal-setting is more effective than having goals dictated by a supervisor.

62. D: Ratio of net income (before interest and taxes) to interest expenses. Liquidity is an organization's ability to meet immediate or short-term obligations as they become due. Measures of liquidity include current ratio, which is the ratio of current assets to current liabilities, and the more stringent acid-test ratio, which is the ratio of current cash and near-cash assets to current liabilities. Unlike the current ratio, the acid-test ratio does not include inventory or prepaid expenses when calculating assets. Accounts receivable turnover is another measure of liquidity and shows the relationship between credit sales and average accounts receivable. Another measure of liquidity is inventory turnover, which is the ratio of the cost of goods sold to average inventory. Ratio of net income (before interest and taxes) to interest expenses, however, is a measure of solvency, rather than liquidity. It demonstrates an organization's ability to meet its long-term obligations and fixed expenses.

63. C: Displays the number of defects in a product over time. Charts and graphs are conceptual tools managers use to assess and improve quality control. A run chart uses horizontal X and vertical Y axes to plot measurements taken over specific intervals, with measurements (amount of product, for example) usually plotted on the Y axis, and time (in intervals of hours, days, weeks, etc.) plotted on the X axis. A histogram, also known as a bar chart, shows the frequency of a particular measurement in a class of measurements. Classes are measured on the X axis, and the number of occurrences is measured on the Y axis. A Pareto chart, as referenced in this question, shows the number of defects or problems in a product over time by using bars of varying lengths. A scatter diagram is a chart in which plotted points indicate the relationship (or lack of one) between two characteristics or events (for example, the relationship between number of cars sold and day of week).

64. D: TQC assumes that a permanent level of quality can be achieved (FALSE). Statistical process control (SPC) uses statistics to monitor and chart processes in order to control variations. SPC assumes that, because nature is imperfect, variations will indeed occur. More comprehensive than SPC, total quality control (TQC) seeks to attain customer satisfaction by integrating quality control throughout an organization, from design to delivery. Because customer perceptions of quality are ever-changing, *a permanent level of quality is not attainable*, according to Armand Feigenbaum, who popularized the concept of TQC in the mid-1950s.

65. A: Functional organization. In a functional organization, specialized activities such as accounting, marketing, production, and the like are departmentalized, with each department (e.g., accounting) serving the entire organization. So, a functional organization would be the type most likely to have a central marketing department. In a divisional organization, each division has its own departments of marketing, production, accounting, etc., so there may be several accounting departments, for example, within one organization. A network organization is a flexible, collaborative relationship among independent firms to produce goods or services. The network organization itself has no traditional hierarchy or organization chart. The dynamic network, also called a virtual corporation, is an extremely flexible kind of network organization in which member-partners can be added or removed as needed.

66. B: They wait to be told what to do. A successful organization needs effective followers as well as strong leaders. Effective followers are those who are willingly influenced by a leader to channel their self-interests toward the goals of the organization. The most effective followers recognize their role and are committed to the organization's vision and mission. *Rather than passively wait to be told what to do, good followers take initiative and are capable of managing themselves.* They seek to increase their skills not only for their own benefit but to further organizational goals.

67. D: 5. Six Sigma is an approach to quality control that was developed in the manufacturing division at Motorola in the 1980s. However, Six Sigma seeks to improve capability and reduce the defects in any organizational process, not only production. Sigma is the Greek letter that represents a standard deviation in statistics, so Six Sigma literally means six standard deviations and indicates how often a defect is likely to occur in a process. Defects generally are measured as DPMO, or defects per million opportunities. The lower the standard deviation, the more defects; the higher the standard deviation, the fewer defects. A Three Sigma process, for example, would have nearly 67,000 DPMO, or roughly a 97 percent accuracy rate. A Four Sigma process would have about 6,200 DPMO, a 99 percent accuracy rate, which seems admirable until one considers the consequences of the defective 1 percent. For instance, a Four Sigma process would result in 20,000 lost postal items an hour or 200,000 wrong prescriptions a year. In some situations, 99 percent simply isn't good enough. A Five Sigma process results in 233 DPMO, and at the Six Sigma level, a process results in fewer than 3.4 DPMO.

68. A: Assets = Liabilities + Stockholders' equity. A balance sheet is a quantitative statement that shows an organization's financial situation at any particular time. It includes assets (whatever the company owns that has monetary value), liabilities (whatever the company owes to its creditors), and stockholders' equity (whatever has accrued to the company's owners). The assets must equal the liabilities plus the stockholders' equity. Balance sheets not only give an organization a snapshot of where it stands at the moment but can help it identify trends and thus strategize for the longer term.

69. B: Buffering. A domain is defined by an organization's competitive boundaries and answers the questions "What industry are we in?" and "Where do we do business?" Although technology has blurred the lines between industries (computers and telecommunications, for example), defining its domain helps an organization to better identify competitors, as well as threats and opportunities. An organization changes its domain by expanding into another industry or market, or leaving an industry or market. Buffering is a way to regulate the flow of production and can occur at either the input or output stage. A company that stockpiles materials needed for production is buffering at the input stage, as with this hardwood flooring company's stockpiled shipment of Brazilian cherry. A company that delays releasing its finished products into the marketplace is buffering at the output stage. Smoothing is a form of control that seeks a steady demand for goods or services. Pricing is a common way to smooth demand: When demand for a product is high, higher prices can decrease the demand; when demand is low, lower prices may increase demand. Rationing seeks to maintain efficiency and the productive use of time, and is used primarily by service providers. The manager of an auto repair shop, for example, rations time and labor by making appointments so the work is spread out during the day. All the above are internal strategies intended to help an organization reduce environmental uncertainty.

70. C: Want to work. In his book *The Human Side of Enterprise*, McGregor propounded two theories of employee motivation: Theory X and Theory Y. Theory X takes an essentially negative view and asserts that people are lazy, don't like to work, don't care about the organization, want little responsibility, and work only for the money and security a job provides. Theory Y, on the other hand, takes a more positive view of people, maintaining that they want to work, can be self-motivated, may seek fulfillment through work and are capable of assuming responsibility and being committed to organizational goals. Proponents of Theory Y, therefore, would begin by assuming that employees *want* to work.

71. A: Maslow's hierarchy of needs. Like Abraham Maslow's hierarchy of needs, Clayton Alderfer's ERG theory describes human motivation in terms of needs. However, Alderfer proposed three primary needs—existence, relatedness and growth, in ascending order—rather than the five espoused by Maslow. Existence needs are basic survival needs (food, clothing, shelter); relatedness needs are based on social relationships; and growth refers to humankind's need to learn and be creative. Unlike Maslow, Alderfer maintained that more than one need may be operating at any one time. In addition to the three needs, the ERG theory advanced the concept of frustration regression—that is, regression toward a lower need when a higher need cannot be met. For instance, a person with an unmet social need may turn to a basic survival need, such as eating, to compensate. In his two-factor theory, Frederick Herzberg proposed that people are affected on the job by two main categories: hygiene factors and motivators. Hygiene factors are characteristics of the workplace, including pay, coworkers, and the like, while motivators are characteristics of the job, including its potential for advancement, the work itself, and so on. David McClelland's learned needs theory maintains that needs are learned, or transmitted through a society's culture. McClelland also emphasized the importance of achievement, affiliation, and power as motivators. J. Stacy Adams' equity theory states that workers not only assess the fairness of their own outcomes (pay, advancement, etc.) in relation to their inputs (contribution of time, talent, etc.) but compare their inputs and outcomes to those of coworkers.

72. B: More task-oriented than relationship-oriented. Fred Fiedler proposed the concept of least preferred coworker (LPC) as a means of identifying whether a leader's style is task-oriented or relationship-oriented. He developed a questionnaire that measures a leader's attitude toward the follower he likes the least (the LPC), which also indicates the leader's attitude toward people in general. The more favorable a leader's responses are about his LPC, the higher the leader's score; the more negative the leader's responses, the lower the score. Fiedler believed that leaders with higher LPC scores cared more about good interpersonal relations and were thus more relationship-oriented than task-oriented. Those leaders with low LPC scores cared less about interpersonal relations and were more focused on getting the job done and thus were more task-oriented than relationship-oriented.

73. C: Parallel team. Work teams are among the most basic in any organization and are designed to accomplish fundamental, clear-cut tasks such as assembling, manufacturing, servicing, etc. Membership in these well-defined teams tends to be stable and consistent. Project and development teams are composed of experts who work together on a specific long-range project, such as a new product. Once the goal is accomplished, the team is dissolved. Parallel teams are temporary teams that operate outside the normal structure. The team is made up of members from different segments of the organization who attempt to find solutions to a specific problem, as with the temporary team in this question. A task force is an example of a parallel team. A management team directs and coordinates the groups under its control.

74. B: A highly cohesive group with low-performance norms. Cohesiveness refers to the group's ability to attract, retain, and influence its members. High cohesiveness not only increases member satisfaction but generally improves performance. Highly cohesive groups are better than noncohesive groups at ensuring that its members perform to the group standard. From management's point of view, this is a two-edged sword. A highly cohesive group with high-performance norms is the highest-performing group possible. However, a highly cohesive group with low-performance norms is the worst-performing group from management's point of view—even though the group attains its goal (of performing poorly). A noncohesive group with high-performance norms can be effective from management's viewpoint, although members acting as individuals likely won't be as effective as if they acted as a team. Yet even a noncohesive group with *low* performance standards isn't as disastrous, from management's viewpoint, as a cohesive group with low standards because the noncohesive group simply isn't as effective at performing poorly.

75. A: Accommodation. Ways of dealing with conflict involve two key behaviors: cooperation, or a willingness to cede to the other person, and assertiveness, or an insistence on one's own interests. Accommodation is cooperating with the other party without being assertive or advancing one's own interests. Avoidance involves denying or minimizing a conflict while doing nothing to satisfy either party. Competing occurs when both parties insist on their own interests and make no attempt to cooperate. Compromise is when neither party is overly cooperative or assertive, with the outcome being moderately satisfactory to both, and collaboration seeks the highest satisfaction for both parties by emphasizing cooperation and assertiveness.

76. C: Budgeting. The four traditional functions of management are planning, organizing, leading, and controlling—*not* budgeting. Planning is identifying the organization's goals and how they will be achieved. Organizing is assembling and coordinating the resources—human, financial, natural, etc.—needed to achieve the organization's goals. Leading is the attempt to motivate and encourage employee performance. Controlling is monitoring performance and making changes as needed.

77. A: Establishing decision criteria. The steps in decision-making typically are: identifying and defining the problem, establishing decision criteria, weighing the criteria, developing alternative solutions, evaluating the alternatives, making a decision, implementing the decision, and evaluating the decision. Criteria form the boundaries for a decision and may include cost, size, and efficiency. Limitations on criteria shrink the boundaries of what constitutes an acceptable decision. The magnitude of the problem also influences what criteria will be established. Weighing criteria is the process of ranking the different criteria in terms of their importance—some criteria will have more weight than others. The bookstore manager opening a new section of gifts and non-book items, for example, will have to decide not only how much space to allot to the section, but its location in the bookstore, what products it will feature, what products will be displaced to what new location, and more. Developing alternatives involves considering other solutions to the problem. If the bookstore manager is opening a gift-card section as a means to draw new customers, perhaps another way would be more effective. Those alternatives are developed, and then evaluated, as part of the decision-making process.

78. C: Delphi technique. Certain techniques allow a group to propose more creative solutions to a problem and reach a better decision. In brainstorming, the group is encouraged to offer as many ideas as possible without any judgment or criticism attached. The ideas aren't evaluated until the session is over. Nominal group technique (NGT) is a structured form of brainstorming that encourages contributions from everyone, even those who are reticent or think better in silence. The technique involves a facilitator, who states the subject or issue and asks members to write down as many ideas as possible within a given time. Each member then states one of his ideas, which may or may not be from his written list, and the facilitator records the ideas on a chart or slide. The ideas are discussed one at a time and then prioritized, with results tallied. The Delphi technique was developed in the 1950s by the RAND Corporation and *uses questionnaires to solicit the opinions of* *experts.* This approach consists of two or more rounds. In the second round, the experts are given the results of the first so they can alter their original judgments if they desire. The survey is done anonymously, and after two or three rounds, a final report is compiled that summarizes the judgments of the Delphi group. In business, the synergistic effect—also known as synergism—is the interaction between two or more parts of an organization that produces an effect greater than the sum of the parts' individual effects.

79. C: Product champion. Effective management of technology is vital to the success of today's organizations. The chief information officer (CIO) is a corporate executive in charge of managing the organization's information technology (IT) group, as well as implementing technological strategy and development across the organization. A technical innovator is someone who develops, or has the skills to implement, a new technology. He may not have the skills or position necessary to promote the technology, however, and so must rely on a *product champion, who—often at the risk of his standing in the organization—promotes the technology* and is, in effect, an in-house PR person for it. An executive champion is someone at the corporate level who embraces the technology and has the authority and resources to get it on track while protecting the product champion.

80. C: It restricts calculated risk-taking. Empowerment is the process of sharing power with employees, which leads to greater involvement in their work, increased confidence in their ability to do their work, and higher morale and the belief that they are an integral part of the organization. Because employees are more involved in their work and have greater decision-making power, fewer supervisors are then needed to monitor and coordinate their activities, thus reducing costs. Although employees are given general direction about overall strategy ("The customer always comes first," for example), they are allowed to make immediate decisions with that strategy in mind. Because employees are given the latitude to make such decisions and act on them, empowerment actually *increases—not restricts—calculated risk-taking*, which pays off in savings of time and money, as well as increased customer satisfaction.

81. A: Productivity is more greatly influenced by psychological and social factors than by physical working conditions. The Hawthorne Studies were conducted in the 1920s and '30s at a Western Electric plant outside Chicago to examine the effect of changing working conditions on productivity. In the first phase, lighting for a test group was increased, and productivity increased. However, the productivity of the control group, whose lighting had not been changed, increased as well. The test group's lighting was then decreased. Surprisingly, productivity increased for both the test and control groups. Another experiment involved an incentive-based, piecework system, which was expected to increase production. But rather than work speedily as individuals, the workers paced themselves as a group, with slower employees decried as "chiselers" and faster employees denounced as "rate busters." Researchers thus concluded that increased productivity was not caused by changing physical conditions or financial incentives but partly by the experiments themselves. The special attention convinced workers of management's interest, which raised morale and led to increased productivity. The term "Hawthorne effect" now refers to the phenomenon in which subjects in behavioral studies change their performance in response to being observed. Thus, productivity was influenced more by psychological and social factors than by objective physical working conditions.

82. A: Fair Labor Standards Act: In *1938, the Fair Labor Standards Act created two categories of employees: exempt and nonexempt.* Managers usually are considered exempt employees—that is, they are salaried employees who are exempt from overtime pay. Employees who are paid hourly are considered nonexempt, and they must be paid for overtime if they work more than 40 hours in a given week. The Civil Rights Act prohibits discrimination in employment based on race, sex, color, religion, or national origin. The Equal Pay Act prohibits pay discrimination based on gender when two jobs are essentially similar, and the Age Discrimination in Employment Act restricts mandatory retirement and prohibits discrimination based on age for people over 40 years old.

83. A: Risen faster than wages and salaries. *The costs of benefits have risen faster than wages and salaries during the past two decades* and today make up a greater percentage—typically about 30 percent—of total payroll than ever before. The primary culprit is the skyrocketing cost of medical care, which affects health insurance benefits. Medical and hospital insurance, as well as pension plans, are optional benefits, and an employer is not required by law to provide them. Benefits required by law are worker's compensation, unemployment insurance, and Social Security. Although employers are trying to rein in the costs of benefits, employees are realizing that compensation includes more than a paycheck.

84. B: At least 30 percent. Typically, workers who are considering joining a union would invite a union representative or organizer to discuss the benefits of unionizing. The union representative then would distribute cards to authorize an election on whether to unionize. If *at least 30 percent* of a company's workers sign the authorization cards indicating they want an election, then the National Labor Relations Board (NLRB) would hold an election by secret ballot on whether to certify the union to represent the company's workers. A simple majority of those voting determines the winner.

85. C: It violates the contract between a union and management. During contract negotiations, which typically occur every three years, workers may go on strike to strengthen their position and persuade management to meet their demands. This bargaining tool is known as an economic strike and is permitted by law. The other kind of walkout is a *wildcat strike, an unplanned stoppage of work that violates the contract between management and the union*. Arbitration—the process of having a neutral third party resolve any disputes over contract interpretation—is designed to head off wildcat strikes.

86. B: Brown v. Board of Education. In Roe v. Wade (1973), the US Supreme Court upheld Jane Roe's claim that her right to privacy entitled her to an abortion, although the court then went on to set certain broad limits to that right. In Brown v. the Board of Education of Topeka (1954), the Supreme Court ruled that separate but equal is inherently unequal and that such *segregation was, therefore, unconstitutional*. The court urged schools to develop desegregation plans. The Dred Scott Decision (1857) ruled, in part, that people of African descent brought into the United States and held as slaves were not protected by the Constitution and could never become US citizens. (As an aside, the court misspelled the defendant's name as Sandford.) In NAACP v. Alabama (1958), the court ruled that Alabama's demand for NAACP membership lists violated the freedom of association guaranteed by the First Amendment.

87. C: Liable should a lawsuit be filed. *Quid pro quo* ("this for that") sexual harassment is when a supervisor or person in a position of authority insists on sexual favors from an employee in exchange for getting or keeping a job or advancing up the corporate ladder. The other, less overt kind of sexual harassment occurs when a hostile work environment is allowed or encouraged. Generally, a hostile environment is one in which women or other protected classes (the disabled, members of certain races, etc.) are subjected to conduct or behavior that is unwelcome or offensive. Thus, repeated racial or ethnic slurs may constitute a hostile work environment. A sexually hostile environment may include a pattern of obscenities, sexual joking, viewing Internet pornography, and the like. Although such behaviors might not be directed at anyone in particular, they create a hostile environment. *A supervisor who allows such behavior on a consistent basis—even if he does* *not participate—may still be held liable,* along with the company, for not preventing or correcting the situation. It is important to note that same-sex harassment falls under the purview of "hostile work environment."

88. B: Homogeneous. A monolithic organization contains few people from different cultural groups and thus has low structural integration. By definition, *a monolithic organization would be homogeneous*—having the same or similar type of people throughout—rather than heterogeneous. A pluralistic organization includes people of different cultural groups and attempts to be inclusive and so is assuredly not monolithic. A multicultural organization also contains and values many cultural groups. Although a monolithic organization may well be parochial—that is, believing its way is the only way—its identifying characteristic is its homogeneity with most, if not all, of its members being of similar race, gender and, perhaps, class.

89. A: Encouraged to keep working. An employee with AIDS falls under the Americans with Disabilities Act (ADA) and therefore must be accommodated in the same way as any employee with a disability. Not only is an employee with AIDS permitted to work as long as he wishes and is able, but he should be encouraged to work and, if possible, offered various options such as telecommuting or flexible scheduling.

90. B: Multinational companies pursue strategies that differ from country to country. The phrases multinational company (MNC) and global corporation sound similar, but they are not interchangeable. A multinational company may be viewed as a domestic firm that does business in two or more countries. An MNC may have subsidiaries in countries where the parent company does business, and those subsidiaries are able to respond to local conditions. *An MNC can thus customize its goods and services and pursue different strategies, country by country.* A global corporation has corporate headquarters and manufacturing facilities throughout the world, which it views as a single market. Because it perceives itself as serving one market rather than many, its goods and services tend to be standardized rather than customized.

91. B: A limit on the profit that a company may return to its home country. A limit on the import or export of certain goods is a quota, and a ban on the import or export of certain goods is an embargo. A tax on imported or exported goods is a duty. *A limit on the profit that a foreign-based company can return to its home country is an exchange control.* All of these are protectionist actions that nations may take as part of their foreign and economic policies. Whether such trade regulations are politically motivated or not, organizations doing business internationally must consider them in their planning.

92. C: Do you have any children? Supervisors and others who screen job applicants should be aware of state and federal laws governing recruiting and employment opportunities. Federal laws are enforced by the Equal Employment Opportunity Commission (EEOC) and, in general, prohibit questions concerning age, race, national origin, sexual preference, religion, disabilities, or marital or parental status. For instance, rather than ask "What is your nationality?" an interviewer might ask "Are you authorized to work in the US?" *To ask "Do you have any children?" or "Do you celebrate Yom Kippur?" is illegal,* but it is legal to ask "Are you available to travel or to work any day or shift?" And although it is illegal to ask an applicant if he ever has been arrested (an arrested person being presumed innocent until found guilty), it is legal to ask if he has ever been convicted. When asking about drug use, an interviewer must be careful to ask about illegal drugs only and not about legal drugs (including alcohol) or prescribed medications, which are covered under the Americans with Disabilities Act. In short, questions should be related to the job itself and the applicant's ability to perform it.

93. D: A supplier of hops. Organizations must deal with an external environment that includes direct and indirect forces. Direct forces are those that immediately affect an organization on a daily basis and include employees, suppliers, customers, and competitors. A supplier of hops would be a direct force that might affect a brewery. Indirect forces have neither an immediate nor daily effect. Several types of indirect forces can influence an organization: social-cultural (e.g., lifestyle changes); economic (e.g., unemployment rates); global (e.g., tariffs); technological (e.g., robotics), and political-legal (e.g., corporate responsibility).

94. B: Securities and Exchange Commission. The Federal Aviation Administration (FAA) regulates civil aviation in the United States and aims to provide the safest, most efficient aerospace system in the world, according to its mission statement. Some of its responsibilities include issuing and enforcing safety regulations and operating airport towers and control centers. The FAA also assigns airspace and controls air traffic. The mission of the Securities and Exchange Commission (SEC) is to protect investors; maintain fair, orderly, and efficient markets; and facilitate capital formation. In its role of protecting investors, *the SEC would investigate complaints regarding executives' compensation and perks.* The National Transportation Safety Board (NTSB) is responsible for investigating civil transportation accidents, including accidents involving aircraft, as well as certain highway crashes, marine and railroad accidents, and pipeline incidents. Upon request, the NTSB also assists the military with certain investigations. The mission of the Environmental Protection Agency (EPA) is, quite simply, to protect human health and the environment. It does so by issuing and enforcing regulations based on US law. These are only four of the scores and scores of US regulatory agencies that can impact an organization.

95. B: Growth is slow and products are not well differentiated. It is management's responsibility to identify its company's competitors and the tactics they are using (e.g., price cuts, a media blitz, etc.). *Competition is likely to be most intense in mature industries where growth is slow or stagnant,* especially if a number of companies provide similar products or services. Newer industries experiencing rapid growth offer many more opportunities, especially if competitors can differentiate their products from one another's.

96. B: Its transportation costs. An organization's culture is, in a sense, its personality. Although, like a personality, somewhat indefinable, organizational culture includes the assumptions, shared beliefs, and values of its members, and can be observed in the way members interact and pursue organizational goals. Even the way members dress or decorate their offices is telling of an organization's culture. The way an organization perceives itself—and seeks to be perceived by others—is a cultural clue also evident in its mission statement. The "legends" and stories about events and characters—past and present—indicate the values and personal characteristics esteemed within the organization. The way the organization treats its employees—whether handing out Christmas bonuses or pink slips—also says worlds about its culture. Although one conceivably could discern aspects of culture based on how a company spends its money, *transportation costs generally wouldn't be a strong indicator of company culture.*

97. C: European Union. The World Trade Organization (WTO) was established in 1995 in Geneva, Switzerland, to help producers of goods and services conduct business internationally. Global in scope, its duties include: administering WTO agreements, which are negotiated and signed by most of the world's trading nations; providing a forum for trade negotiations; and handling trade disputes. The Asia-Pacific Economic Cooperation (APEC) was established in 1989 to facilitate economic growth, cooperation, trade, and investment in the Asia-Pacific region. Unlike the WTO, APEC requires no treaty obligations; decisions are reached by consensus. *The European Union (along with its currency, the euro) was created by the Maastricht Treaty,* which was signed in Maastricht, the Netherlands, in 1992. The EU's goal is to create an economic superpower capable of competing with the United States. The North American Free Trade Agreement (NAFTA), which took effect in 1994, eliminated trade barriers among the United States, Canada, and Mexico, creating the world's largest free-trade area.

98. B: Insourcing. Outsourcing, which is also called contracting out, involves hiring an outside provider or manufacturer to produce goods or services in order to cut costs. Offshoring is the transfer of work to foreign countries in order to take advantage of relatively cheap labor. Many concerns have been raised about job losses due to offshoring and, in particular, outsourcing. Nonetheless, evidence suggests that since the beginning of the 21st century, most US manufacturing jobs have been lost not because of offshoring or outsourcing, but because of technological advances and innovations, which allow more efficient production of goods with fewer workers. Insourcing—the opposite of outsourcing—is the term for the transfer of jobs or operations within a country, either by hiring local subcontractors or building a production facility. Toyota's assembly plant in San Antonio, Texas, is an example of insourcing, which *creates* US manufacturing jobs, rather than causing a decline.

99. C: Franchising. Managers face five choices when deciding to expand overseas: exporting, licensing, franchising, joint ventures, or wholly owned subsidiaries. Exporting (producing goods at home and then shipping them abroad) is usually the first step in global expansion. It offers economies of scale and low risk. With international licensing an organization grants a foreign company the right to manufacture its product in the foreign country. The foreign company (licensee) bears most of the costs and risks of opening up the new market. Franchising is similar to licensing but is used primarily by service companies rather than manufacturing firms. In international franchising, the franchisor grants the foreign franchisee the right to use the company name. The franchisee agrees to run its company in a manner identical to the franchisor's, whose brand name is on the line. *Quality control can become a major issue if the franchisee does not meet the franchisor's standards.* Because the brand name is the same everywhere, a slip in quality in one place affects the franchisor's reputation worldwide. An international joint venture—a popular way to enter foreign markets—occurs when a company forms a new entity with a foreign company, with both contributing capital and sharing in revenue and expenses. Wholly owned subsidiaries are independent foreign companies owned by the parent company, which bears all the risks and costs of setting up the foreign company.

100. D: 55 and older. According to employment projections by the Bureau of Labor Statistics, the fastest-growing segment is workers age 55 and older, who are expected to represent more than 20 percent of the labor force by 2014. Overall, the US civilian labor force is growing more slowly than in the past, largely because the number of workers age 16 to 24 is declining. Management must pay attention to such demographics, which have an impact on recruiting and retention of employees.

How to Overcome Test Anxiety

Just the thought of taking a test is enough to make most people a little nervous. A test is an important event that can have a long-term impact on your future, so it's important to take it seriously and it's natural to feel anxious about performing well. But just because anxiety is normal, that doesn't mean that it's helpful in test taking, or that you should simply accept it as part of your life. Anxiety can have a variety of effects. These effects can be mild, like making you feel slightly nervous, or severe, like blocking your ability to focus or remember even a simple detail.

If you experience test anxiety—whether severe or mild—it's important to know how to beat it. To discover this, first you need to understand what causes test anxiety.

Causes of Test Anxiety

While we often think of anxiety as an uncontrollable emotional state, it can actually be caused by simple, practical things. One of the most common causes of test anxiety is that a person does not feel adequately prepared for their test. This feeling can be the result of many different issues such as poor study habits or lack of organization, but the most common culprit is time management. Starting to study too late, failing to organize your study time to cover all of the material, or being distracted while you study will mean that you're not well prepared for the test. This may lead to cramming the night before, which will cause you to be physically and mentally exhausted for the test. Poor time management also contributes to feelings of stress, fear, and hopelessness as you realize you are not well prepared but don't know what to do about it.

Other times, test anxiety is not related to your preparation for the test but comes from unresolved fear. This may be a past failure on a test, or poor performance on tests in general. It may come from comparing yourself to others who seem to be performing better or from the stress of living up to expectations. Anxiety may be driven by fears of the future—how failure on this test would affect your educational and career goals. These fears are often completely irrational, but they can still negatively impact your test performance.

Elements of Test Anxiety

As mentioned earlier, test anxiety is considered to be an emotional state, but it has physical and mental components as well. Sometimes you may not even realize that you are suffering from test anxiety until you notice the physical symptoms. These can include trembling hands, rapid heartbeat, sweating, nausea, and tense muscles. Extreme anxiety may lead to fainting or vomiting. Obviously, any of these symptoms can have a negative impact on testing. It is important to recognize them as soon as they begin to occur so that you can address the problem before it damages your performance.

The mental components of test anxiety include trouble focusing and inability to remember learned information. During a test, your mind is on high alert, which can help you recall information and stay focused for an extended period of time. However, anxiety interferes with your mind's natural processes, causing you to blank out, even on the questions you know well. The strain of testing during anxiety makes it difficult to stay focused, especially on a test that may take several hours. Extreme anxiety can take a huge mental toll, making it difficult not only to recall test information but even to understand the test questions or pull your thoughts together.

Effects of Test Anxiety

Test anxiety is like a disease—if left untreated, it will get progressively worse. Anxiety leads to poor performance, and this reinforces the feelings of fear and failure, which in turn lead to poor performances on subsequent tests. It can grow from a mild nervousness to a crippling condition. If allowed to progress, test anxiety can have a big impact on your schooling, and consequently on your future.

Test anxiety can spread to other parts of your life. Anxiety on tests can become anxiety in any stressful situation, and blanking on a test can turn into panicking in a job situation. But fortunately, you don't have to let anxiety rule your testing and determine your grades. There are a number of relatively simple steps you can take to move past anxiety and function normally on a test and in the rest of life.

Physical Steps for Beating Test Anxiety

While test anxiety is a serious problem, the good news is that it can be overcome. It doesn't have to control your ability to think and remember information. While it may take time, you can begin taking steps today to beat anxiety.

Just as your first hint that you may be struggling with anxiety comes from the physical symptoms, the first step to treating it is also physical. Rest is crucial for having a clear, strong mind. If you are tired, it is much easier to give in to anxiety. But if you establish good sleep habits, your body and mind will be ready to perform optimally, without the strain of exhaustion. Additionally, sleeping well helps you to retain information better, so you're more likely to recall the answers when you see the test questions.

Getting good sleep means more than going to bed on time. It's important to allow your brain time to relax. Take study breaks from time to time so it doesn't get overworked, and don't study right before bed. Take time to rest your mind before trying to rest your body, or you may find it difficult to fall asleep.

Along with sleep, other aspects of physical health are important in preparing for a test. Good nutrition is vital for good brain function. Sugary foods and drinks may give a burst of energy but this burst is followed by a crash, both physically and emotionally. Instead, fuel your body with protein and vitamin-rich foods.

Also, drink plenty of water. Dehydration can lead to headaches and exhaustion, especially if your brain is already under stress from the rigors of the test. Particularly if your test is a long one, drink water during the breaks. And if possible, take an energy-boosting snack to eat between sections.

Along with sleep and diet, a third important part of physical health is exercise. Maintaining a steady workout schedule is helpful, but even taking 5-minute study breaks to walk can help get your blood pumping faster and clear your head. Exercise also releases endorphins, which contribute to a positive feeling and can help combat test anxiety.

When you nurture your physical health, you are also contributing to your mental health. If your body is healthy, your mind is much more likely to be healthy as well. So take time to rest, nourish your body with healthy food and water, and get moving as much as possible. Taking these physical steps will make you stronger and more able to take the mental steps necessary to overcome test anxiety.

Mental Steps for Beating Test Anxiety

Working on the mental side of test anxiety can be more challenging, but as with the physical side, there are clear steps you can take to overcome it. As mentioned earlier, test anxiety often stems from lack of preparation, so the obvious solution is to prepare for the test. Effective studying may be the most important weapon you have for beating test anxiety, but you can and should employ several other mental tools to combat fear.

First, boost your confidence by reminding yourself of past success—tests or projects that you aced. If you're putting as much effort into preparing for this test as you did for those, there's no reason you should expect to fail here. Work hard to prepare; then trust your preparation.

Second, surround yourself with encouraging people. It can be helpful to find a study group, but be sure that the people you're around will encourage a positive attitude. If you spend time with others who are anxious or cynical, this will only contribute to your own anxiety. Look for others who are motivated to study hard from a desire to succeed, not from a fear of failure.

Third, reward yourself. A test is physically and mentally tiring, even without anxiety, and it can be helpful to have something to look forward to. Plan an activity following the test, regardless of the outcome, such as going to a movie or getting ice cream.

When you are taking the test, if you find yourself beginning to feel anxious, remind yourself that you know the material. Visualize successfully completing the test. Then take a few deep, relaxing breaths and return to it. Work through the questions carefully but with confidence, knowing that you are capable of succeeding.

Developing a healthy mental approach to test taking will also aid in other areas of life. Test anxiety affects more than just the actual test—it can be damaging to your mental health and even contribute to depression. It's important to beat test anxiety before it becomes a problem for more than testing.

Study Strategy

Being prepared for the test is necessary to combat anxiety, but what does being prepared look like? You may study for hours on end and still not feel prepared. What you need is a strategy for test prep. The next few pages outline our recommended steps to help you plan out and conquer the challenge of preparation.

Step 1: Scope Out the Test

Learn everything you can about the format (multiple choice, essay, etc.) and what will be on the test. Gather any study materials, course outlines, or sample exams that may be available. Not only will this help you to prepare, but knowing what to expect can help to alleviate test anxiety.

Step 2: Map Out the Material

Look through the textbook or study guide and make note of how many chapters or sections it has. Then divide these over the time you have. For example, if a book has 15 chapters and you have five days to study, you need to cover three chapters each day. Even better, if you have the time, leave an extra day at the end for overall review after you have gone through the material in depth.

If time is limited, you may need to prioritize the material. Look through it and make note of which sections you think you already have a good grasp on, and which need review. While you are studying, skim quickly through the familiar sections and take more time on the challenging parts.

Write out your plan so you don't get lost as you go. Having a written plan also helps you feel more in control of the study, so anxiety is less likely to arise from feeling overwhelmed at the amount to cover.

Step 3: Gather Your Tools

Decide what study method works best for you. Do you prefer to highlight in the book as you study and then go back over the highlighted portions? Or do you type out notes of the important information? Or is it helpful to make flashcards that you can carry with you? Assemble the pens, index cards, highlighters, post-it notes, and any other materials you may need so you won't be distracted by getting up to find things while you study.

If you're having a hard time retaining the information or organizing your notes, experiment with different methods. For example, try color-coding by subject with colored pens, highlighters, or post-it notes. If you learn better by hearing, try recording yourself reading your notes so you can listen while in the car, working out, or simply sitting at your desk. Ask a friend to quiz you from your flashcards, or try teaching someone the material to solidify it in your mind.

Step 4: Create Your Environment

It's important to avoid distractions while you study. This includes both the obvious distractions like visitors and the subtle distractions like an uncomfortable chair (or a too-comfortable couch that makes you want to fall asleep). Set up the best study environment possible: good lighting and a comfortable work area. If background music helps you focus, you may want to turn it on, but otherwise keep the room quiet. If you are using a computer to take notes, be sure you don't have any other windows open, especially applications like social media, games, or anything else that could distract you. Silence your phone and turn off notifications. Be sure to keep water close by so you stay hydrated while you study (but avoid unhealthy drinks and snacks).

Also, take into account the best time of day to study. Are you freshest first thing in the morning? Try to set aside some time then to work through the material. Is your mind clearer in the afternoon or evening? Schedule your study session then. Another method is to study at the same time of day that you will take the test, so that your brain gets used to working on the material at that time and will be ready to focus at test time.

Step 5: Study!

Once you have done all the study preparation, it's time to settle into the actual studying. Sit down, take a few moments to settle your mind so you can focus, and begin to follow your study plan. Don't give in to distractions or let yourself procrastinate. This is your time to prepare so you'll be ready to fearlessly approach the test. Make the most of the time and stay focused.

Of course, you don't want to burn out. If you study too long you may find that you're not retaining the information very well. Take regular study breaks. For example, taking five minutes out of every hour to walk briskly, breathing deeply and swinging your arms, can help your mind stay fresh.

As you get to the end of each chapter or section, it's a good idea to do a quick review. Remind yourself of what you learned and work on any difficult parts. When you feel that you've mastered the material, move on to the next part. At the end of your study session, briefly skim through your notes again.

But while review is helpful, cramming last minute is NOT. If at all possible, work ahead so that you won't need to fit all your study into the last day. Cramming overloads your brain with more information than it can process and retain, and your tired mind may struggle to recall even previously learned information when it is overwhelmed with last-minute study. Also, the urgent nature of cramming and the stress placed on your brain contribute to anxiety. You'll be more likely to go to the test feeling unprepared and having trouble thinking clearly.

So don't cram, and don't stay up late before the test, even just to review your notes at a leisurely pace. Your brain needs rest more than it needs to go over the information again. In fact, plan to finish your studies by noon or early afternoon the day before the test. Give your brain the rest of the day to relax or focus on other things, and get a good night's sleep. Then you will be fresh for the test and better able to recall what you've studied.

Step 6: Take a Practice Test

Many courses offer sample tests, either online or in the study materials. This is an excellent resource to check whether you have mastered the material, as well as to prepare for the test format and environment.

Check the test format ahead of time: the number of questions, the type (multiple choice, free response, etc.), and the time limit. Then create a plan for working through them. For example, if you have 30 minutes to take a 60-question test, your limit is 30 seconds per question. Spend less time on the questions you know well so that you can take more time on the difficult ones.

If you have time to take several practice tests, take the first one open book, with no time limit. Work through the questions at your own pace and make sure you fully understand them. Gradually work up to taking a test under test conditions: sit at a desk with all study materials put away and set a timer. Pace yourself to make sure you finish the test with time to spare and go back to check your answers if you have time.

After each test, check your answers. On the questions you missed, be sure you understand why you missed them. Did you misread the question (tests can use tricky wording)? Did you forget the information? Or was it something you hadn't learned? Go back and study any shaky areas that the practice tests reveal.

Taking these tests not only helps with your grade, but also aids in combating test anxiety. If you're already used to the test conditions, you're less likely to worry about it, and working through tests until you're scoring well gives you a confidence boost. Go through the practice tests until you feel comfortable, and then you can go into the test knowing that you're ready for it.

Test Tips

On test day, you should be confident, knowing that you've prepared well and are ready to answer the questions. But aside from preparation, there are several test day strategies you can employ to maximize your performance.

First, as stated before, get a good night's sleep the night before the test (and for several nights before that, if possible). Go into the test with a fresh, alert mind rather than staying up late to study.

Try not to change too much about your normal routine on the day of the test. It's important to eat a nutritious breakfast, but if you normally don't eat breakfast at all, consider eating just a protein bar. If you're a coffee drinker, go ahead and have your normal coffee. Just make sure you time it so that the caffeine doesn't wear off right in the middle of your test. Avoid sugary beverages, and drink enough water to stay hydrated but not so much that you need a restroom break 10 minutes into the test. If your test isn't first thing in the morning, consider going for a walk or doing a light workout before the test to get your blood flowing.

Allow yourself enough time to get ready, and leave for the test with plenty of time to spare so you won't have the anxiety of scrambling to arrive in time. Another reason to be early is to select a good seat. It's helpful to sit away from doors and windows, which can be distracting. Find a good seat, get out your supplies, and settle your mind before the test begins.

When the test begins, start by going over the instructions carefully, even if you already know what to expect. Make sure you avoid any careless mistakes by following the directions.

Then begin working through the questions, pacing yourself as you've practiced. If you're not sure on an answer, don't spend too much time on it, and don't let it shake your confidence. Either skip it and come back later, or eliminate as many wrong answers as possible and guess among the remaining ones. Don't dwell on these questions as you continue—put them out of your mind and focus on what lies ahead.

Be sure to read all of the answer choices, even if you're sure the first one is the right answer. Sometimes you'll find a better one if you keep reading. But don't second-guess yourself if you do immediately know the answer. Your gut instinct is usually right. Don't let test anxiety rob you of the information you know.

If you have time at the end of the test (and if the test format allows), go back and review your answers. Be cautious about changing any, since your first instinct tends to be correct, but make sure you didn't misread any of the questions or accidentally mark the wrong answer choice. Look over any you skipped and make an educated guess.

At the end, leave the test feeling confident. You've done your best, so don't waste time worrying about your performance or wishing you could change anything. Instead, celebrate the successful completion of this test. And finally, use this test to learn how to deal with anxiety even better next time.

Review Video: Test Anxiety
Visit mometrix.com/academy and enter code: 100340

Important Qualification

Not all anxiety is created equal. If your test anxiety is causing major issues in your life beyond the classroom or testing center, or if you are experiencing troubling physical symptoms related to your anxiety, it may be a sign of a serious physiological or psychological condition. If this sounds like your situation, we strongly encourage you to seek professional help.

Online Resources

Due to our efforts to try to keep this book to a manageable length, we've created a link that will give you access to all of your online resources:

mometrix.com/resources719/dsstprsuper

It's Your Moment, Let's Celebrate It!

Share your story @mometrixtestpreparation